THE
BEGINNER'S
GUIDE TO
INSIGHT
MEDITATION

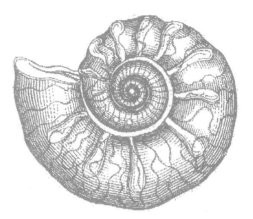

THE BEGINNER'S
GUIDE TO
INSIGHT
MEDITATION

ARINNA WEISMAN
AND JEAN SMITH

BELL TOWER  NEW YORK

Acknowledgments appear on page 230.

Published by Bell Tower, New York, New York
Member of the Crown Publishing Group.

Random House, Inc. New York, Toronto, London, Sydney, Auckland
www.randomhouse.com

Printed in the United States of America

Design by Barbara Sturman

Library of Congress Cataloging-in-Publication Data
Weisman, Arinna.
The beginner's guide to insight meditation / Arinna Weisman and Jean
Smith—1st ed.
Includes bibliographical references and index.
1. Meditation—Buddhism.   2. Spiritual life—Buddhism.
3. Buddhism—Doctrines.   I. Smith, Jean, 1938–   II. Title.
BQ5612 W4   2001
294.3'4435—dc21

ISBN 0-609-80647-5

10 9 8 7 6 5 4 3 2 1

First Edition

To my students, who have inspired me so much with their courage and efforts, and to my teachers for their purity and wisdom — AW

For all my teachers — JS

Contents

Preface

WE HOPE THIS BOOK touches that part of you which has longed for freedom but hasn't given it a name and which has yearned for lasting happiness but hasn't thought it possible. We hope this book provides a gateway through which you meet these yearnings, entering the world of the Dharma, the Buddha's teachings.

One of the remarkable aspects of Insight Meditation—also known as *Theravada* ("Teaching of the Elders") Buddhism, or *Vipassana* ("insight meditation," in the Pali language of the Buddha's time)—is that this path is very simple. It is not always easy, but it is possible. Although no one can know when the results of a spiritual path will manifest, we can be certain that the efforts described here, in honor of our heart's liberation, will bear fruit. May we find

> Grace to live with an open heart and humor amid the
> turbulence of life's changes
> Presence that illuminates our lives and guides us in truth
> Compassion to hold all life's pain and suffering

NOTE: In general, Pali rather than Sanskrit terms have been used, except when Sanskrit terms—for example *sutra (sutta), Nirvana (Nibbana), Dharma (Dhamma)*—are more commonly used in the West.

THE
BEGINNER'S
GUIDE TO
INSIGHT
MEDITATION

1. The Possibility of Change: A Cinderella Story

When I was a child, the Cinderella story made me distinctly uncomfortable. So did Anne of Green Gables. *Here were these images of people who were just too good to be true: They were generous, they were sweet, they were diligent, they worked hard, they were compassionate, they never seemed angry or judgmental or shaming or hating. At some level, I longed to be like them, but I felt that I was more like Cinderella's ugly sisters: They were jealous of each other, they were nasty, they were competitive, and they were social climbers. They thought that they were not good enough, and yet they were self-consciously proud. Not until many years later did I learn that within the practice of Insight Meditation I could embrace such seemingly contradictory feelings with peace and even affection. — AW*

Many people experience this rift within themselves. Sometimes we feel anger, jealousy, envy, and desire like Cinderella's ugly sisters, who will eventually be relegated to the dim kitchen in the Prince's palace or to a dark place in our hearts. At the same time, we yearn to have the qualities of Cinderella and the Prince—beauty, virtue, generosity—and to live happily ever after. The good news is that no matter how powerfully we may feel torn between such conflicting feelings, the Buddhist tradition known as *Insight Meditation*, or *Vipassana*, invites us to heal that division.

Insight Meditation teachings do not demand that we live life as an eternal bliss trip by judging or cutting off what feels difficult or negative. That is simply not a realistic expectation for any human being. Instead, when energies such as anger, hatred, doubt, and anxiety—traditionally called the *hindrances* in this practice (chapter 3)—arise, we can learn to hold them in our hearts with kindness and with acceptance. We acknowledge them and even honor them, saying, "Aha, here are these energies inside me. May I hold them with kindness. May I hold them with softness." That conscious relationship—it is like Cinderella and the ugly sisters merged—is where transformation happens.

If we could not envision how we would like to live and if we did not have the perseverance to make that vision a reality, we could not change. One of our greatest advantages as human beings is that as long as we are alive, we *can* change.

This capacity feels to me like such a critical piece because when I was growing up I was not very happy. I was quite shut down and judgmental. I'm not saying this out of any sense of shame—it is just a pure acknowledgment of how I was, of how unhappy I was. If it were not for the possibility of change, I would still be caught in those negative energies. — AW

Even though we sometimes feel as if we are being clutched by hurtful energies, the fundamentally good part of our nature is always there and can be awakened. The heart of Insight Meditation calls upon our inner potential for wisdom, kindness, illumination, and a deep sense of connection to the beauty of all life. When this potential unfurls without obstruction, we are free—free of suffering, living with happiness that is not dependent on any particular thing, experience, or circumstance. This is our possibility. It is not just theoretical or something we are asked to accept on blind faith. Proof of it exists in the lives of our spiritual teachers and people such as the Buddha, Mahatma Gandhi, Hildegard of Bingen, Nelson Mandela, Aung San Suu Kyi, and the Dalai Lama.

Nelson Mandela elegantly invited us to express our possibility in his 1994 inaugural speech as president of South Africa.

Our deepest fear is not that we are inadequate.
Our deep fear is that we are powerful beyond measure.
It is our light, not our darkness, that most frightens us.
We ask ourselves, Who am I to be brilliant, gorgeous,
    talented, and fabulous?
Actually who are you not to be?
You are a child of God. Your playing small does not serve
    the world.
There is nothing enlightened about shrinking so that
    other people will not feel insecure around you.
We were born to manifest the glory of God that is
    within us.
It is not just in some of us; it is in everyone.
And as we let our own light shine, we unconsciously give
    other people permission to be the same.
As we are liberated from our own fears, our presence
    automatically liberates others.

The Nature of Suffering in Our Lives

Insight Meditation teachings recognize the challenges we face in living as human beings and the reality that we often experience pain and sometimes tremendous suffering. Suffering does not mean we are failures or awful persons or should feel ashamed about what is happening to us. The process of healing begins when we acknowledge our suffering and explore it, when we admit what is happening—and accept it.

As we open to our lives, we face the difficulty of illness. Some of us lose our health in a permanent way, for example, through cancer, heart disease, or arthritis. We all undergo the process of aging. Our bodies disintegrate in different ways and at different rates, but the changes due to aging are unavoidable and often painful. And we will all die—a scary prospect for many of us.

For some of us, our deepest challenges may be not physical but emotional, as psychic wounds keep opening up and bringing suffering. Even when no great difficulties are confronting us, a general sense of dissatisfaction may permeate us. We may believe things are going well, but we may still feel unfulfilled, or that we are not living our deepest purpose, or even that our life is out of control.

The Buddha said that we cannot deny these difficulties. It would be foolish and unrealistic to even try, for we would just be repressing a part of ourselves. Insight Meditation is not about repression; nor is it about splitting ourselves off from ourselves or pretending to be some sort of perfect spiritual model that excludes half of our lives. This practice, rather, is about relating to ourselves as we are. It is about saying, "Okay, let me find a way to work with these difficulties. How do I do that?" The Buddha said, "This is the way," and he laid out teachings so that we could live with the challenges of life and still find happiness. The teachings are revolutionary because they acknowledge our difficulties and in doing so inspire us to embrace a spiritual practice that can bring us peace.

You may have picked up this book because you know, at some level, that this is the moment for you to seek your spiritual truth. Or perhaps your life partner just died, you lost a job that was very important to you, or you have developed a chronic physical disability or experienced some other huge challenge. You say to yourself, "I know I cannot pretend this did not happen. Of course it happened. But how do I live with peace and equanimity? How can I live with kindness to myself?" Within Insight Meditation practice there are answers to these kinds of questions.

Our first step together could be to take the *Refuges*.

The Three Refuges

Over the centuries many people seeking the path of awakening, happiness, and freedom have begun their commitment by a practice known as taking the *Three Refuges*. But this practice is much more than a historical ritual. It is an affirmation of our capacity to change. It acknowledges, first, that there is a possibility of our awakening; second, that there is a way of living or practicing that can create the conditions for this awakening; and third, that we are not alone in this endeavor—we are joined and supported by thousands of other beings and communities.

Some phrases for taking the refuges are:

May I take refuge in my capacity to awaken.
May I take refuge in the ways of living that bring about
my freedom and happiness.
May I take refuge in those who are fully awakened and
feel open to all those who can support me on this
path of freedom.

Taking the First Refuge means taking refuge in our fundamental *Buddha-nature,* with its potential for *enlightenment.* Taking the Second Refuge means taking refuge in the teachings that awaken this nature (known as the *Dharma*). Taking the Third Refuge means taking refuge in those who are fully awakened and opening to the community that practices together (known as the *Sangha*), which provides a resting place that is safe, nourishing, and transformative.

We often find ourselves taking refuge in other things that we think are going to bring us happiness. We have been taught that happiness comes about through having, owning, and accumulating. If we have a serviceable car, we might still find ourselves desiring a better model. We may wish for a new house, longer vacations in more beautiful places, or better relationships. These things are not bad, but they do not bring lasting happiness. A lasting happiness is one that illuminates our being whether we have a nice car or not, better furniture or not, a longer vacation or not. This possibility of achieving a lasting happiness that is not dependent on any thing or circumstance is called our fundamental nature, or Buddha-nature.

Taking the First Refuge means acknowledging that we have the capacity to be happy in this way. It is a treasure we carry in our hearts, more valuable, the Buddha said, than the most precious jewels in the world, than all the treasures of royalty. This happiness is not born of greed or hatred. It is not the kind of happiness someone might feel if they have longed for something and through treachery finally gotten it. It is not the kind of happiness people feel who gain power over others and can make them do exactly what they want. This kind of happiness, rather, comes from deep kindness and respect for all beings and all life. It comes with a clear wisdom that always sees what is skillful, appropriate, timely, and true. This happiness lives in a heart that has no boundaries of "us" and "them" but comes through our intimate connection with all of life. It is a happiness that expresses being at peace. It is a happiness that comes from being present in each moment. This happiness is our possibility, and the refuges remind us that we *can* find it.

The First Refuge acknowledges the beautiful part of our being and encourages us to say, "No matter what I have done or said or thought, no matter what my job is, no matter whether I'm married or have children or not, whether I think I'm a failure or a success, no matter *what*, I have this capacity inside of me for transformation, and it can bring lasting happiness." Immediately, our relationship to ourselves changes. We enter into a relationship of honor and respect with ourselves by affirming our fundamental nature. Each time we take the First Refuge, we connect with the possibility of transformation.

The Second Refuge—taking refuge in the Dharma—is the refuge of training ourselves to see clearly how things are. In this clarity there is no conflict, confusion, or suffering. Just as a mirror reflects back whatever image is in front of it at that moment without picking and choosing, we can train ourselves to see how things are without the personal distortions of our projections, desires, aversions, or stories. Insight Meditation calls this type of seeing *wisdom*, and wisdom is not distant or cold. On the contrary, the space created when we let go of our attachments brings a heart that is vast in its kindness. Without our personal prejudices and attachments, we develop a natural friendliness and contentment toward all our experiences and for all beings. Taking refuge in the Dharma supports our development of wisdom and compassion.

The Buddha taught only what was helpful in finding the truth through this refuge—he was not interested in obtuse theories. So taking refuge in the Dharma is a straightforward practice of cultivating what brings happiness and renouncing what brings suffering. Through it we can create the conditions for lasting transformation where all obstacles to freedom disappear.

Finally, the Third Refuge—taking refuge in the Sangha— affirms that we are not alone, that many thousands of beings like us have the same questions and the same search and are attempting to live in freedom. Originally the word *Sangha* referred to the fully enlightened disciples of the Buddha in his lifetime, but today, in Insight Meditation, we refer to both formal and informal communities, including our teachers, as Sanghas (see chapter 10).

We can also extend Sangha to include all of life. When we are drinking a cup of tea, we can feel we are with sangha, with the water that nourishes us, the fire that heated the tea water, and the earth where the tea was grown and from which the cup took form. The universe joins us in drinking the tea. We are all in communion. Walking along in a daydream, we hear a bird call, and it brings us back to being present with ourselves, so we could say that the bird is also part of the sangha supporting our practice.

Exercise: Taking Refuge

The Buddha did not demand that we become Buddhists or renounce our other religious practices. His teachings do not require our unquestioning obedience. Rather, the Three Refuges involve strengthening our intentions to let go of suffering and to cultivate happiness. Would you like to take the refuges?

Spend a few moments considering your intentions, then take the refuges formally, using the phrases at the beginning of this section, or others that express your intentions, or the traditional phrases for taking the Three Refuges:

> I take refuge in the Buddha.
> I take refuge in the Dharma.
> I take refuge in the Sangha.

If you would like to, bring your palms together with your fingers pointing to your chin at the level of your heart while you say the refuges.

You can take the refuges as many times as you like during the day and/or at the beginning of your meditation practice (chapter 2).

2. Meditation: The Path to Transforming Our Lives

I squirmed. I itched. My knees hurt. My left foot was asleep. My mind was bouncing around all over the place, from memories of my tenth-grade science teacher to daydreams of a vacation in Paris I hoped to take someday. I felt as though I would jump out of my skin if it were not so miserably tight. Sharon Salzberg and Joseph Goldstein, the teachers for my first Insight Meditation workshop, had given fairly detailed instructions for how to sit and maintain focus on the breath, but my experience was bearing little resemblance to the quiet state they described. Finally, sometime during the second day, I raised my hand and wailed, "I do not know why you call this Insight Meditation. I can't tell which is more uncomfortable—my body or my mind—I'm constantly shifting one or the other to try to avoid pain. My mind is like a monkey swinging from tree to tree. Where is the insight?"

Joseph smiled and quietly said, "You've just described it." — JS

Insight is the ability to see clearly, to see things as they really are. The fuel that feeds insight is *mindfulness,* or awareness, which we cultivate through the practice of *meditation.* Mindfulness, when it is supported by other qualities, can both free us from suffering and bring us to a deep sense of unity and well-being at our most basic level. When we meditate, we can see how our mind works and how we react—such as the insight that by pushing away and avoiding discomfort, we close down our hearts. Joseph Goldstein's teacher once told him, "If you want to see how the mind works, sit down [meditate] and watch it."

When the Buddha looked into the human mind, he determined that it is made up of fifty-two energies. Some of these energies bring happiness and some do not; they are described in traditional Buddhist discourses as *skillful* and *unskillful* mental qualities. These teachings do not make a moral judgment about ourselves as good or evil—they simply affirm that some qualities in our minds have the power to bring transformation from suffering and some do not. We already know this from our own personal experience. Diligence, patience, and generosity bring us the conditions for happiness. Jealousy, envy, laziness, and not having any sense of what hurts ourselves or others—so-called immorality—do not.

The Buddha noted that the possibility of transforming ourselves rests in our intentions to awaken and in our understanding of what we can do and how we can do it. The cultivation of skillful mental energies most serves our intentions for true healing. These energies—primarily mindfulness—bring about the opening of our inner nature so we can rest in peace and unity.

Mindfulness

Often I take some time at the end of the day to go for a walk along the quiet street where I live. Lovely oak trees line the road, and between them you can see the sky, sometimes clear and deep blue, sometimes dark and overclouded. I walk back and forth, using the movement of my body and the feeling of my feet touching the ground to bring my mind to balance and to let go of the worries that have a way of niggling into oneself.

One evening I found myself thinking about one of my sisters. I had sent her a birthday present, and she had not called to say thank you, which hurt me. I began to think, "How come she never calls back? She is impossible. She never reaches out to me," and so on. Right then I recognized that I was creating a whole story out of one fact: She had not called. The story involved not only these thoughts but a whole series of feelings that were very familiar—feelings of being ignored or invisible.

This moment of clarity allowed me to make a choice. Did I want to spend my time on this beautiful evening with these thoughts? No, I would much rather enjoy being present with the trees, the quiet, and my body moving. I saw I could choose to reinforce these feelings by believing them and building up a sense of myself as unrecognized, or I could drop the thoughts. It was such a clear choice and a profound gift to be able to see how I was creating suffering and separation for myself, then to let this pattern go and continue walking. (It turned out that my sister had been very grateful for the present but hadn't been able to call right away because her daughter was in an accident.) — AW

Each of us is presented with the same kind of choice many times in our daily lives. But only the clear seeing of mindfulness gives us the opportunity to opt for serving our happiness and rejecting negative habitual mind patterns, which bring us so much suffering.

Much of how we are, what we think, and how we express ourselves is an accumulation of different messages and experiences that are unconsciously inherited from the past. We find ourselves continuing to act out of them regardless of whether they serve us well. Our morning ritual, for example, might be getting up when the alarm clock goes off, throwing the covers over the bed, brushing our teeth, and stumbling into the shower after we put on the kettle and turn on the radio or TV. We make a telephone call while drying ourselves, sipping our tea, and half-listening to the morning news. We skim the newspaper while eating breakfast. Through this whole sequence, we might not be present—we do not actually know what we are doing. In this relationship of not knowing, we take actions and say things, carried along by the momentum of habit and doing. The Buddha used the phrase *wheel of samsara* to describe this mind*less* involvement in our lives—all the things that we do over and over again without awareness and love. Developing mindfulness gets us off automatic pilot and enables us to be present for our lives.

With mindfulness, we can observe whether our lives meet our heart's desire for a deep happiness. In the seeing, we can decide whether to continue our habitual ways or to change them. A life lived without mindfulness may be compared to an African pond that is so entirely covered by a nonnative species of water lily the water is not visible. It is impossible to tell that the natural quality of water is refreshing, translucent, and cleansing, reflecting how things are. In the same way, the habitual patterning of our lives—with entwined "lily pads" of suffering—obscures the beauty of our underlying nature. But when we choose over and over again to live connected to the moment and aware of what we are doing, we begin to weed away that covering. We start to live increasingly with the depth, clarity, and illuminated quality of what water—and our inner nature—is actually like.

So, you might ask, what has all this to do with meditation? Here is the crux of why we meditate: *We meditate in order to cultivate the skillful qualities of mind—particularly mindfulness.*

Mindfulness is presence of mind or attentiveness to present experience without "wobbling" or drifting away from it. Like a mirror, mindfulness reflects what is happening without the distortion of our old ideas, habit patterns, or prejudices. Rather, it sees our experience clearly and directly. Viewing our experience mindfully is not like looking through the wrong end of a telescope, so that things appear very far away and small. Mindfulness does not have that sense of separation, or dualism. When we are mindful, we are actively and intimately participating in the experience.

In his discourses, the Buddha described two kinds mindfulness: bare attention and general comprehension. Imagine standing in a garden, looking at a red rose, and really seeing it—the color, and how it deepens at the base of the petals, the particular way the petals are opening, the form and shape they give to this flower. *Bare attention* is the quality of mindfulness that sees the details of an experience without labels, projections, or interpretations. We see the color and form of the rose without ever using the label *rose.* Or, for example, in the next moment we can hear a sound of ringing and listen to it without immediately overlayering the experience with the label *church bells.*

Now, open to the understanding that you are standing in a

garden having seen a red rose and having listened to church bells with bare attention. This is *general comprehension*, which has the quality of understanding the whole situation, including the purpose of what we are doing. In this instance, we comprehend that we have been practicing bare attention and that this skillful activity is part of the spiritual practice that opens our hearts and minds.

We can practice developing mindfulness—and other skillful qualities—at any moment in our lives, but setting aside specific time to cultivate it is extremely effective. Many people have found that unless they reserve such time, it is difficult—especially in the beginning—to develop this quality. Cultivating mindfulness through meditation is like cultivating physical fitness. You go to the gym, where you exercise in order to strengthen and train your body, so that you will be strong no matter where you are. In the same way, you can create particular spaces and times in your life to train in mindfulness. At the gym, when you are training your body, that is the only thing you are doing—you are not driving a car or reading or eating. The same is true for awakening and strengthening mindfulness meditation. The Buddha said that we can meditate in any position—sitting, standing, walking, or lying down. In this chapter, we will begin with mindfulness training through sitting and walking meditation.

Sitting Meditation

One boon of Insight Meditation practice, in contrast to some other spiritual traditions, is that it is not a fixed set of rules. Instead, individual practice is founded on each person's self-inquiry into what works for them. Here is one set of guide-

Meditation Each retreatant in the Spirit Rock meditation hall has chosen the meditation posture that works best for her or him. Postures shown in this chapter include sitting in the Burmese posture (front left), on the *seiza* bench (center), riding the horse (front right), and sitting in a chair (back).

lines, but others are also possible. See if they are helpful—that investigation itself is part of Insight Meditation practice. Sitting practice is a fundamental piece of this tradition, but in the context of our daily life, we need to be flexible. Sometimes when we go through serious emotional or physical trauma or physical illness, sitting meditation does not work. Then we have to find other ways to cultivate mindfulness, such as walking meditation, described later in this chapter, and practices such as the divine abodes, described in chapter 9.

PLACE

It is helpful but not critical to find a quiet space where you can meditate regularly. If you live in an environment that is not so quiet, that is fine—you can incorporate the sounds into your meditation practice. Some people find it very grounding to create a special altar area where they sit; others sit in the middle of their bed. The most important thing about place is for you to really *be* wherever you are.

TIME AND FREQUENCY

If you can sit every day, once or twice a day, the benefits are tremendous: It tends over time to bring about a profound transformation in your life. But do not judge yourself if you cannot sit this often, because punishing yourself is *not* part of this practice.

Some people like to sit soon after they awaken, perhaps setting their alarm early and even bunching up pillows so they can sit before they get out of bed. Others cannot sit first thing in the morning because they have children to feed or animals to walk; the only time possible for them may be at night. Many people who have long, intense workdays also find night an

Home Altar Many meditators find it helpful to set up a meditation area in a quiet part of their home where they meditate daily.

ideal time to meditate and become quiet before they go to bed. According to your schedule and your life, see what time works for you.

Assign yourself a goal to meditate for a certain length of time. You might want to sit for ten, fifteen, or twenty minutes as a beginning. It is important not to assign such an unrealistically long time that you set yourself up for failure. You can always lengthen the time as your practice deepens. What is critical in the beginning is to say to yourself, "Okay, even if I get the urge to jump up ten times during these next fifteen minutes, I'm going to persevere in sitting here for the full time." An important factor in being able to sit for the full time is to find a comfortable posture.

POSTURE

Two particularly helpful suggestions regarding posture are, first, find a position in which you can relax and, second, keep your back relatively upright. You *could* meditate lying down— some people do so for health reasons—but it is more challenging not to fall asleep. It is also true that many of us have meditated with bent backs, so it is not a set rule that you cannot meditate unless your back is absolutely straight.

In Insight Meditation, we meditate with our eyes lightly closed so that we will not be distracted by what is around us. If you are feeling particularly sleepy, you can open your eyes slightly, looking downward about three feet in front of you. Other schools of Buddhism, such as Zen, meditate with open eyes.

The traditional meditation position in Theravada Buddhism is to sit on the floor (or on a mat called a *zabuton*) in a *full lotus posture*, in which each foot, sole upward, is placed on the thigh of the other leg. Most of us are not flexible enough to do that,

The Full Lotus   Statues of the Buddha most often show him in the full lotus posture, in which each foot is placed, sole upward, on the opposite thigh. In this *mudra*, or hand position, the Buddha-to-be invokes the Earth to witness his right to seek enlightenment, a moment described on page 48.

The Half Lotus   In the half lotus posture, one foot, sole upward, rests on the opposite thigh while the other foot rests on the floor near the pelvic area.

The Burmese Posture   In this posture, the meditator sits on the floor or the front third of a cushion with legs folded, but not crossed, in front of the pelvic area.

so we find alternatives. In the *half lotus posture*, which also demands considerable flexibility, the heel of one foot is tucked toward the pelvic area and the other foot rests on the thigh of the opposite leg. It is far more common—and for most people, more comfortable—to sit on a cushion (a *zafu*) in the *Burmese posture*, with the the pelvic area and the other leg folded in front of it, but not on top of it or crossing it.

If you are using a cushion, sitting on the front third will help you keep your back straight. Some people also put small pillows under their knees. In an alternative called *riding the horse*, you kneel, place the cushion on edge between your legs, and sit back on it. If sitting on a cushion is not comfortable for you, you might also try using a

Riding the Horse The meditator turns the cushion sideways and sits back on it.

***Seiza* Bench** The meditator sits on the bench with legs folded underneath.

Sitting in a Chair Meditators may find sitting on a chair the most comfortable posture. It may be helpful to sit away from the back of the chair with a straight back, and a cushion may be used under the feet so that the thighs are at a right angle to the body.

three-piece bench called a *seiza bench*, which also helps keep the back erect. If none of these options is comfortable for you, *sitting in a chair* is fine. You might find it useful, for keeping alert, to sit erectly without resting against its back. It is neither more holy nor more beneficial to sit on the bare floor, or on a cushion or a bench, than in a chair, so whatever is comfortable *and* supports your being alert is the position you should choose. Two final notes on comfort: Some people have found it helpful to wear trousers or skirts that are loose enough to allow them to hold a posture without binding. Also, sometimes we become chilled as we sit, so you might want to keep a shawl or light blanket nearby that you can put around your shoulders or over your legs.

A Guided Sitting Meditation

It is often helpful to frame a sitting with a statement of your intentions. See if you would like to begin this meditation by connecting with your intention to support skillful qualities of mind, to be kind to yourself, to be patient with yourself, to be present with yourself in a nonreactive way, to be aware. Perhaps you would like to call something else into being. The important thing is to be clear about *what* you are doing and *why* you are doing this meditation. (This is what we mean by cultivating general comprehension, page 15.) If it is helpful for you, you can phrase the intention as taking a refuge: "I understand that I am doing this to awaken my potential nature for wisdom and happiness, my fundamental nature of goodness. And I dedicate myself to practicing patience, perseverance, and effort in this endeavor."

Let your eyes close gently.

Invite your body to relax and release into the support being given by the ground, chair, or cushion. You can let go of your tensions or sense of doing. This time of meditation is itself often a refuge. You are offering yourself a quiet space from your hectic life. Once again invite yourself to let go into that support. There is no need to insist that you relax or let go. Offering the invitation is enough.

Acknowledge, if you are sitting, the uprightness of your upper body—you may already be feeling some tightness in your shoulders or around the jaw. See if it is possible to acknowledge these tensions without trying to change them. You are not trying to change your experience—just to be present for how it is, just to know it.

You may want to take a moment to acknowledge the places in your body where you feel physical sensations clearly—perhaps the place where your buttocks are resting on your cushion or chair and the sense of pressure where your feet are touching the ground.

Then open to the feelings of your breath as the air moves in and out of your body. Become sensitive, inviting the quality of "listening in" to the experience as your awareness knows the sensations. Can you feel the coolness of the air as it passes through the nostrils, or perhaps just a sense of the movement of air in and out? Perhaps there is a tingling or vibration there. Can you feel the rising and falling of the chest or abdominal region? Other sensations you might feel in this region are stretching, pulling, pressure building and releasing. Allow your attention to settle where you feel the breath most clearly—in the nostril region, the chest, or the abdomen. That is the place to focus your attention while you meditate.

We have a tendency to want the breath to be a particular way, especially if we have done yoga, in which breathing is the practice rather than the object of the practice. If you become aware of this urge, notice that desire but see if you can allow your breath to be as it is, in the same way you might observe the sun rising and setting, just one of the natural phenomena of life. There is no right breath or wrong breath. It might be deep or shallow, coarse or smooth. However it is, it is just fine. You are cultivating a relationship of allowing and knowing the experience, not of controlling it. When you notice you are controlling the breath, see if you can stay with the sensations of the tightness in the breath without reacting or interpreting.

Again and again invite yourself into the relationship of allowing the breath, the natural movement of life in our bodies, to be as it is. Can you know your breath fully? Can you drop everything else and give full attention to the whole breath: just the breath and your knowing of it, from the very beginning of the inbreath through to the end of the outbreath? Notice if there is a space between the end of the inbreath and the beginning of the outbreath, or between the end of the outbreath and the beginning of the next inbreath. See when the next inbreath comes—just one breath at a time.

The mind has a tendency—and you will notice this many times—to go off into thinking. Thinking is not an enemy, but your habitual thinking is simply not helpful in this transformative process. So for now, see if you can drop the thinking process and come back to the breath. You will find that your mind will go back into thinking almost immediately again. Consider awareness of one whole inbreath and one outbreath quite an accomplishment. Meditation is about letting go of our thinking mind over and over again, then coming back to the breath. It does not matter how long we have been caught up in our thoughts; we can always begin again. Beginning again is an important part of this practice and is one of the great "muscle builders" of mindfulness.

When other physical sensations become dominant—for example, sharpness, itching, or some other strong discomfort in the body—acknowledge them. You are not actually pushing them away but rather discerning them. You might, for example, explore what the actual experience of pain is. When you let go of the concept "pain," what is there? Heat, pulsing, throbbing? Is it the same in the middle as at the outer edges? Can you begin to distinguish the difference between the unpleasant quality of the experience and the physical sensations? If you continue to be aware of the sensations, how do they change? If aversion or a strong desire to "get rid of" the pain arises, then go back to the breath or investigate a "safer" part of the body. You can also examine strong emotions in the same way, acknowledging them, then coming back to the breath, using the breath as an anchor, a place to keep returning to. (We will look specifically at other difficulties that may arise during sitting in chapter 3.)

At the end of fifteen or twenty minutes, or however long you set for yourself, take a moment to appreciate your efforts and to honor the intention to meditate. You have given a special gift to yourself, as well as to everyone else. The Buddha said that we can give ourselves no gift—no amount of money, jewels, or material beauty—that is greater than cultivating mindfulness and kindness.

Walking Meditation

Walking can be another wonderful opportunity to cultivate mindfulness. Movement can strengthen our awareness, and it is sometimes a more accessible object for meditation than the breath.

Formal walking meditation techniques vary in different streams of Theravada Buddhism. In some Buddhist traditions, meditators walk in a line or a circle. In the Burmese tradition and on Insight Meditation retreats, meditators usually walk alone. The invitation is to walk back and forth between two points twenty to thirty feet apart, which helps us to let go of the need to "get somewhere." *We practice walking just to walk.* Choosing a place to practice at the beginning of the walking period also eliminates spending most of the time making that decision. Try to stick to your chosen place, because you may be confronted with desires such as "This place is too noisy. I should walk around the back of the building." But the back area turns out to be too cold, so you have to search for a warm spot. But alas, to your horror, the only warm area is filled with other people and you cannot do walking meditation unless you are alone. By now thirty minutes have gone by, so you decide to give up. Knowing in advance where you will walk eliminates this fruitless indecision.

When you have selected your place, divide the walking meditation into three parts. During the first part, perhaps ten or fifteen minutes long, walk a little more slowly than you would normally. During the second part, which is also ten to fifteen minutes long, slow down even more. In the third, the remaining time you walk, move very, very slowly.

It is also fine, instead of breaking your walk into three stages, to choose one of the paces and walk back and forth at that speed. As in all practices in Insight Meditation, whatever feels appropriate to you, given the conditions, is what you should do.

A Guided Walking Meditation

Begin, as you did with sitting meditation, by acknowledging your intention and your commitment to cultivating mindfulness through this practice.

In the first segment of your walking meditation, allow your awareness to focus on the sense of stepping on the ground. If you would like to bring more energy into your system—and one of the wonderful things about walking meditation is that it actually brings energy into the mind— lift your knees a little bit higher and decrease the stride, so that you are taking shorter steps. Notice the sense of stepping on the earth: *stepping, stepping, stepping.*

In the next portion, slow down enough so that you notice the lifting of the foot and then the stepping of the foot on the ground. *Lifting, stepping—lifting, stepping—lifting, stepping.* You will notice, as with sitting meditation, that the mind wanders many times. No problem. Just keep bringing it back to the sensations of lifting and stepping,

Walking Meditation These retreatants at Spirit Rock choose their outdoor meditation path and walk back and forth between points twenty to thirty feet apart.

and to the knowing of that sequence. You *know* that you are lifting when you lift, and you *know* that you are stepping when you step.

The last sequence is *lifting, stepping, shifting—lifting, stepping, shifting.* In this segment, slow down enough so that you really notice the shift of weight and pressure from one foot to the other. Notice the details of the experience. Notice that when a foot is lifted up, muscles in your side may be working. Observe how the foot glides across the surface of the ground, how the foot hangs, and then when stepping—do not shift immediately—just acknowledge placing the foot on the ground. Then let the sequence happen again, staying connected to *lifting, stepping, shifting—lifting, stepping, shifting.*

Some people find it helpful to do *noting*—to say descriptive words very softly in their minds as they perform the actions of walking meditation. When they are lifting, they say, "Lifting"; when they are stepping, "Stepping"; when they are shifting, "Shifting." Be careful not to make the words predominant—they should be far in the background—but noting can give you a little extra support in being aware of the walking process and can help keep you focused.

In addition to noting, *walking by counting*—a focus on developing stability and mental concentration—can also assist you when your mind is distracted. In this practice, you can walk at a normal pace. When you take your first step, you count 1. On the next two steps, you say 1, 2. On the next three steps, you say 1, 2, 3. The next four steps are 1, 2, 3, 4 and so on all the way up to 10. When you reach 10, you say 10, then 10, 9 for the next two steps; then 10, 9, 8 for the next three steps, and so on. Whenever you lose your concentration, you go back to 1. What often happens is that when you are in the middle of the sequence and get to 10, you then say 11—you forget to make the transition back because you are not really concentrating: You are on rote. If you want to move your body while focusing your mind, counting is very useful. You can do it in a short space and keep turning around, or you can do it on a long walk by repeatedly starting over again.

When you are walking, your primary focus is on the sensations of walking. Sometimes you will notice that you are focused not on walking but rather on seeing or hearing—a very common experience. When that happens, just note, "Seeing" or "Hearing," and then come back to walking again. If, during formal practice, you *want* to look at something, acknowledge this intention, stop walking, look at what you want to look at, and then continue walking again with your focus on the steps.

Formal walking practice might not fit into your daily life. Perhaps the only time you take a walk is when you take the dogs out in the morning, and there is no way you can be doing *lifting, stepping, shifting*. No problem. Just take a general comprehensive awareness of walking, and notice over and over again how it feels for your body to be moving. Or you might find it easier to focus on the feet, noticing the placing of a foot on the ground, connecting with the earth, and feeling the rhythm of walking. This kind of mindfulness is as valuable as formal walking. One is not better than the other. Both are useful in their own way, so your choice of which one to do depends on the conditions in your own life.

Jogging can become your practice too—feeling the general movement of the body and in particular the rhythm of the feet on the ground. Moving the body either in a certain form such as yoga or from your own internal sense of rhythm can very much be part of your cultivation of mindfulness.

Exercise: Movement Meditation

You can fully experience movement as an object of meditation by focusing on the sensations arising in the body from the movement. If working with the breath or walking meditation is difficult for you, this meditation offers another opportunity to cultivate mindfulness.

Begin by acknowledging your intention to cultivate mindfulness through this practice.

Lie down on a firm surface, such as the floor. Close your eyes lightly. Starting with your feet, invite all the muscles of your body to release into the support underneath them. If you would like, include the weight of the bones in this surrendering into the ground. Continue until the whole body has been invited to release its full weight into the support underneath you. There is no need to insist or demand that the body relax. Offering the invitation is enough.

Allow your head to move very slowly from one side to another so that one ear and then the other is facing the floor. See if you can refrain from pushing or forcing the rotation. It is helpful to think of the movement as your head being moved by itself. You are there to receive the sensations from the movement. So let yourself become very sensitive to the feeling of pressure or tingling or stretching that comes from the movement. A thought may have arisen by now, as in the breathing or walking meditation; let it go when you recognize that you are thinking, and come back to the awareness of sensations through the movement. Allow your jaw to relax again and the sense of contraction that you may find behind your eyes. As long as you feel connected to this movement, keep allowing your head to move and relax into the movement with your awareness.

When it feels right, allow yourself to come to rest, inviting your body once again to relax into the floor. Allow your arm to be moved up toward the ceiling as though a string were attached to the wrist and were pulling the arm up. Let it happen very slowly. Stay connected with the sensations arising from the movement. Allow your wrist and fingers to move in whatever way occurs naturally once your arm is up. Let go of any idea you might have about where the movement should happen, and let it come to you from inside the fingers and wrist. It is fine to remain still and wait for it to happen. When you feel ready, allow your arm to return to the floor. Extend this invitation to the other arm and then to each of your legs. Other movements can be included in this meditation, such as lifting your back off the floor by shifting the weight of your body onto your feet and shoulders or by turning onto your side and lifting your arm and leg facing the ceiling, as we have just described. It is fine to experiment to see what movements work best for you.

When you are ready to end this meditation, see if you would like to acknowledge and appreciate your efforts.

Exercise: Daily Practice

Set aside a period of time each day to practice one of the guided meditations. See if you can do this for a whole week. Then recommit for the next week. If it is easier to commit one day at a time, see if you can begin your day with that intention.

Keep a journal of your experiences. If this is difficult for you to do, take a moment to reflect on your experiences during your meditation practice—the moments of mindfulness, when you forgot, your intentions to come back again, and whatever else stands out for you.

Appreciate your efforts.

3. Difficulties in Meditation—and Life

Several years ago, I decided to spend four days alone with nature, meditating and fasting, so I went off to a wilderness area with some friends who wanted to do the same thing. We had planned to go out for an hour the first morning so that each of us could find our individual sacred spot, where we would spend these days alone. Unfortunately for me, the area my friends had chosen was heavily forested. I'm someone who loves open space, and I feel crowded and even imprisoned in forests. I could not imagine spending the whole four days deep in the woods. The first day I got up at dawn—I did not take any water or food—to try to find open space somewhere. I walked frantically, here and there, uphill and down, but had no luck. My mind was full of thoughts such as "I am not going to find what I'm looking for. This is awful." I was feeling really attached to discovering the perfect place and at the same time feeling certain that I was *going to fail. I had awakened with a fever that morning, and I could feel my body both sweating and shivering. It was time to go back. I turned around, deeply disappointed, thirsty, and fatigued, and started going to where I thought "back" was. Each tree looked familiar and I thought I recognized the path, but no, that wasn't it. I turned and tried another direction but never found our base camp. Hours later it dawned on me that I was completely lost and that my life was in jeopardy. In that moment I understood I had to surrender—my doubts, my anger, my attachment to finding the perfect place, even to finding the path out. I lay down on a rock by a river and totally let go. I felt the cold hardness of the rock underneath me and heard the gurgling sounds of moving water. A deep peace grew inside me. And then a bolt of clear directed energy pulsed through me saying without words: Get up and go this way. I turned to the west and walked mindfully, feeling each foot stepping on the ground as if drawn along magnetically at each turning. Eventually I got to a road and a cabin, whose owners drove me the long distance back to the base camp.*

I ended up having four wonderful days because I had come to understand the gift of letting go of my attachments and doubts and of surrendering into the moment as it is. — AW

Spending time alone provides a remarkable opportunity to experience the skillful and unskillful qualities of mind introduced in chapters 1 and 2. Both the enriching and the difficult mental energies also can arise dramatically during our meditation practice. This chapter looks at five specific unskillful qualities traditionally called the *hindrances:* desire (for some particular experience), ill will (toward the pain in our leg, for example), sloth and torpor (drowsiness), restlessness (perhaps for the meditation to be over), and doubt (about doing the wrong kind of spiritual practice, for instance). They are called hindrances because they interfere with our ability to come to insight, and sometimes they all come at once in what is known as a multiple-hindrance attack. (For the Buddhist text on the hindrances, see pages 206–208.)

We are often seduced by the hindrances into believing that if we follow these energies, they will bring us happiness—for example, the attachment to open space as the only possibility for a satisfying four days in nature. Our possibility for transformation comes not in repressing these energies or in creating a split between "ourselves" and "them," as in the story of Cinderella and her sisters, but in acknowledging them without identifying with or believing in them. Grappling with the hindrances is not a reason to judge ourselves but rather an opportunity to investigate the energies to see if they lead us toward or away from strengthening our meditation practice and the conditions for happiness.

We need to recognize that the hindrances arise in *all* of us until we are totally free. Our spiritual path is a developmental process—and it is not necessarily neatly linear. It is a journey of purification and cleansing that often lifts our hidden emotions to the surface, especially the negative ones. Such emotions do not mean that we are doing the practice incorrectly. Our practice is actually going quite well when mindfulness illuminates experiences so that they feel stronger than in the normal rhythm of life. Just because meditating may be difficult does not mean that we are not on the right path. Rather, the common difficulties that many of us experience in the beginning—restlessness and not being able to sit still for a minute, being attacked by doubt, pain, or sleepiness, having strong desire or aversion—can be invitations to a spiritual practice.

Sensual Desire

Sensual desire resembles grasping a sticky object. It is as though our world is coated with Krazy Glue and everything we touch clings to us. In our meditation practice, we often become stuck on pleasant physical sensations or experiences. Desire persuades us that if only we had a pleasant breath or a spacious feeling that we had earlier, then we would be happy. But desire is insatiable. As soon as we get the object or experience we have been longing for, we move on to another desire, because the more we pursue desire, the more desire we experience. Fulfillment of desire can never satisfy desire—a fact that turns upside down our cultural "understanding" that we will be happy if only we fulfill sensual desire for pleasant experiences: food, sex, cars, clothes, homes, and on and on.

It is probably accurate to say that we have spent much of our lives pursuing our desires in the hope that once we have obtained satisfaction from them, we will be happy. If this expectation were realistic, then we might expect to find ourselves ecstatically happy much of the time. But it is not, and we are not. Desire blinds us to the truth the Buddha observed, that desire can never bring us lasting happiness. It brings contraction rather than spaciousness, separation rather than connection. It shuts down our hearts rather than opens them. We may even experience such strong desire that we do not care if we hurt someone in the process of fulfilling it.

Desire not only brings contraction and separation but is impossible to always satisfy. We cannot always get the job or house we want. Our children, wives, husbands, partners, parents, and friends are not always what we would like them to be.

To live our lives pursuing the dreams of desires can only bring us suffering.

When I was young, I drove very old, not particularly attractive cars. I wasn't interested in and didn't notice other cars on the road. While I was a university student in my thirties, my little Honda Civic died. Because I was so short of funds, the only way I could get another car was to buy a new one with no down payment at an outrageous interest rate. So I bought a new Toyota Tercel. I liked the design of the car and thought it was pretty cool. Some weeks later, driving down the freeway to class, I noticed I was looking longingly at a Toyota Camry (a much more expensive car). Now that I had a new car, I already wanted a better version! — AW

In our meditation practice, through awareness we can separate desire from its object and examine desire itself. If we desire soft, easy, smooth breaths, we can turn our attention to desire and see how it takes us out of the present moment and into the future. We can feel the contraction and pulling of it, and we can see how it can bring restlessness or doubt and all kinds of thoughts associated with it. This examination can give us exceptional insight as to how desire operates in our life—how it adheres to its object, how it makes its object more attractive than it really is and blinds us to its unattractive aspects. We can examine how insatiable desire is.

When we feel desire, we do not have to judge ourselves. The nature of the untrained mind is to experience desire. Our role is to recognize it, acknowledge it, and let it go, through one of the techniques described below.

Concentration, aiming the mind at the breath or another object of meditation such as lovingkindness, is one antidote to desire. When the mind is steadily connected to the object of our meditation, there is no space for desire to arise. Even if we are not meditating, when we notice desire, we can try to let it go by switching our attention to something else, such as our posture or what we are hearing or seeing, or by just thinking of something else—remaining attentive to this alternative object or experience.

Several other practices can help us work with desire. Contemplating the unattractive aspects of the desired object is effective. We also can give ourselves little talks, such as "It's okay. Desire is just an experience. It's like eating cotton candy—so insubstantial, and afterward there's just an empty feeling."

Faced with desire, we can also contemplate impermanence, the overriding characteristic of life. Failure to acknowledge the truth of change is the greatest source of our suffering, and desire is based on the assumption that things do not change. Most of us have had a moment during meditation when the mind felt open, the breath moved with ease, and there was great concentration. We thought we had finally "gotten it," and this was the way our practice would be. But then our experience changed, and the next meditations were awful. We spent weeks trying to hold on to or recreate that wonderful moment. It was an impossible quest.

In our daily life we can clearly see the interaction of desire and impermanence in our long-term relationships. We meet someone, are filled with desire, and think, "I've found my life partner, and we are the perfect match. This is *it*." At least we feel this way when we first meet the person and perhaps for the first six months or year. But if we stay together for five, ten, or fifteen years, then we increasingly know that intimate relationships are a blend of some blessings and some difficulties, many of them unpleasant. During the difficult times we might even come to the conclusion that "this person has changed and is *not* the right person for me."

When we experience desire as just another passing experience, we can acknowledge it with words such as "Desire, welcome. I see you have come to visit. I know you well. You are a frequent guest. But I am not entering into a conversation with you or getting involved in any of your stories. So you are free to leave at any time." There is no need to struggle.

Powerful desire may be a cover for difficult emotions that we have not acknowledged. When we are caught in a net of desire, it may therefore be helpful to investigate what is going on in our emotional world. It is important to let go of all the thoughts or stories we have about the desire and drop down underneath the conceptual level. If we can let go of agendas such as "I am getting rid of desire by looking at my emotions," our exploration can have an open, listening, kind energy. Try to experience a difficult emotion without identifying with it or becoming lost in it. See if you can hold it with awareness and spaciousness. When we can open to and allow these underlying emotions, we create the conditions for coming back to balance and harmony. With this balance, the strength of the desires begins to evaporate, and we feel released from their grip.

....

Ill Will

Ill will, or aversion, arises when our experiences are unpleasant. It is the opposite of desire. Instead of grasping for something, ill will—including anger, hatred, and fear—pushes it away. When we are meditating, we sometimes find we do not like our breath—it is too short, too shallow, or too rough—or our body feels too hard and heavy, or we feel a horrible pain in our knee. We become critical of what is going on and angry with ourselves because our minds are not calm or because we are trying so hard to meditate and cannot, or with the pain in our knee, which seems to be messing up our meditation. We often think that unpleasant experiences are an expression of some failure on our part or an indication that something wrong has to be fixed. So we keep pushing away or rejecting unpleasant experiences with our ill will.

Can we separate our aversion from what feels like its cause—for example, the pain in our back—and examine it with nonreactive awareness? What is the actual experience of aversion? How does it feel in our body? Is it open or contracted? Does it bring ease or tension? When awareness is strong, just seeing aversion often frees us of its hold—an important function of awareness. If we bring awareness to aversion but find ourselves reacting to it, we can then come back to the breath or to some experience where aversion does not arise. We might, for example, open up to a general sense of our whole body sitting, or to sound, and allow our mind to rest here for a while.

Another classic antidote to ill will is to cultivate an interest in the experience that has triggered it. See if you can separate the unpleasant quality of the experience from the actual physical experience. What is pain? What are its characteristics?

In Insight Meditation healing happens when we cultivate the qualities of mind that allow us to have an experience without judging it. We are in training to be all right no matter what our experience is. This is not to say that there will not be countless times when we will judge the pain in our back or our breath—that is the nature of a wobbly mind—but we will increasingly see clearly that we do not want to go down this route.

The Buddha said in *The Dhammapada*, a collection of his verses (see pages 209–211):

> In this world
> Hate never yet dispelled hate.
> Only love dispels hate.

Lovingkindness thus is one of the main antidotes to ill will because it has the capacity to soften the hardness and release the contraction of aversion. We can call forth kindness to meet difficult experiences with thoughts such as "May this pain be held with kindness." Or we can meet the aversion with kindness as well: "May I hold this aversion with kindness." If we are caught in anger toward another person, we can call forth kindness to that person or direct the formal lovingkindness meditation (*Metta Sutta*) toward him or her (see pages 208–209).

Because it is often difficult to summon lovingkindness when we are feeling ill will, the Buddha suggested that we contemplate the positive qualities of the object or experience.

I sometimes find myself irritated while doing household chores. I think: "How come I am doing these chores again?" I don't find it particularly pleasant to vacuum. I don't like the dust. The vacuum cleaner is heavy and always turns over and gets entangled in the furniture. It is easy in this unpleasantness to start becoming irritated with others in my household for not vacuuming more often. When I notice these thoughts, they are familiar intruders. But then I think of all the other activities my partner has done: built a desk for me, fixed lightbulbs, taken the sink apart when it leaked, and all the other things I never do. I also think about the pleasure of having a vacuum cleaner because I used to live without one and it was really hard to keep the house free of dust. — AW

Cultivating joy is another direct antidote to ill will. If pain in your body has brought up strong aversion, sometimes it is helpful to contemplate the blessings of having a knee, leg, or shoulder—or a whole body—that functions. You can spend some time in this contemplation and every now and again touch those painful sensations lightly with awareness. If aversion to the pain is still there, you can continue to contemplate the blessings of having a body and other blessings in your life. To practice with this kind of patience and perseverance is a tremendous gift to yourself.

If you are caught up in a story about someone and ill will is the related emotion, it is helpful to let go of the story line and come back to the body. Instead of repeatedly "rehearsing" in your mind "what they did to me," you can begin to explore the contraction in your chest, the burning sensation in your throat, the tension in your jaw. We know "our stories" inside out and backward, and thinking about them again does not teach us anything or lead to happiness. If it did, we would all be extremely happy because we spend so much time indulging our stories. We can call on our resources as spiritual warriors to bring forth the energy to drop—and keep dropping—our stories. The healing that happens through letting go of our stories over and over again and coming back to a neutral object such as the breath is profound. Coming back to awareness of a neutral object strengthens awareness, the very quality that can help us to resolve difficult situations.

In dealing with ill will, the Buddha also bade us contemplate his teaching that unskillful actions sow only the seeds of suffering through cause and effect, or *karma* (pages 85–88).

....

Sloth and Torpor

In meditation, drowsiness, feeling heavy, and falling asleep—charmingly referred to in the Buddha's discourses as sloth and torpor—are very common experiences. This state is a dullness of mind, a lack of driving power, in which we feel as though all our energy is dispelled. It has a sinking quality to it. Again, as with desire and ill will, we overcome this difficulty by acknowledging that this is our experience. It is not bad; it is just the experience.

Several antidotes are helpful when you start to feel drowsy:

○ In the beginning, after you have acknowledged drowsiness, do not use it as an object of attention; rather, find a different object.

○ Mentally scan different touch points in the body, such as your shoulders, knees, buttocks, and feet, and for a moment allow your mind to alight at each place. Feel the sensations at each place if they are accessible; if not, just know where your attention is, then move on to the other points. Keep doing this until you feel more alert.

○ Open your eyes and stay either with scanning the body or with the breath.

○ Count your breaths to help stay present. One technique is

to count each inhale up to 5, 7, or 10. You usually will not get all the way up to 5, much less to 10—you will have to keep going back to 1 because you have forgotten to count and have begun thinking. But just bringing in the extra effort of counting is useful.

○ Stand up if you are really falling asleep. Some people have even stood on their heads at the beginning of their meditation in order to change the energy so that they do not sleep.

○ Go for a fast walk.

○ Repeat to yourself what you know of the teachings of the Buddha or your understanding of what brings about your happiness.

Awakening energy by exerting effort to connect with a chosen object such as one on this list is the direct antidote to heavy drowsiness.

....

Restlessness

One morning I sat down to meditate on my bed in a little cabin in the California redwoods. I had just come back from a retreat and was very inspired to sit every day. As I sat, I realized I hadn't set my alarm clock to let me know when twenty minutes was up. I got up, set my alarm, and started to sit again. Then I remembered I had not switched off the phone. I was sure the phone would disturb me, so I'd better turn it off. I jumped off the bed and turned off the phone. When I got back onto the bed, I discovered that I had messed up the particular configuration of pillows that was comfortable, so I had to turn around and get my pillows "right."

I sat down again. I probably felt one breath, then I started to think about some problems at work. In that moment, I thought I had come up with a brilliant solution to a really difficult problem, and if I didn't write it down that very minute, I was going to forget it. So I got up again and wrote down what I thought was the solution. Then I started to think about all the other problems at work. Guess what happened next? The twenty minutes were over, and my alarm went off.

As restless as I was that time, it was nothing compared to my first meditation experiences, when I was like a jumping bean. I could not sit still for a moment. My face was itchy and I had to scratch, and my back was in agony and I had to keep shifting position. My mind was all over the place. — AW

Restlessness is agitation. It is the opposite of a quiet mind. It makes the mind unsteady, and we feel in turmoil, like water whipped by the wind.

When you can, you greatly help your practice by persevering in your commitment to sit and by refraining from jumping up to write something down, to switch the alarm clock on or the telephone off, or to leap onto whatever train of thought arrives to entice you into leaving your meditation. It often feels as though a situation justifies being agitated—for example, worrying about a traffic delay when you have to catch a plane. Restlessness seduces us into thinking that if we are restless enough, we will somehow make things better. It never occurs to us that being agitated or worried contributes nothing at all to improving the situation. Agitation just breeds more agitation.

As with the other hindrances, the invitation here is to separate the anxiety from what we are anxious about and to see it as the hindrance restlessness. We learn to trust that if we let go and direct our minds back to our breath or the posture of our bodies, such as sitting or standing, we become much more effective because we develop steadiness of mind, which sees clearly what needs to be done. This steadiness of mind can also bring happiness, which is a classical antidote to restlessness.

A common attribute of restlessness is *monkey mind*, the tendency of the mind to jump from one thought to another to another. Insight Meditation stresses that we strengthen our practice not by not thinking but by *returning from thinking*. The dazzling solutions and plans that arise during meditation came up the first time and will come up again; we can write them down after our meditation time. Cultivating mindfulness in a moment-to-moment, ongoing way creates transformative insight, something our thoughts cannot do.

Restlessness may also take the form of physical agitation. It is not bad to move during meditation, but you can try not to be mindlessly reactive to physical experiences such as pain or itching. You can recognize them, acknowledge them, and see what they feel like (often, for example, itching involves a sensation of heat), then adjust your posture with as much awareness as you have been giving to your breath.

It is easy to forget that we are training our mind and that, just like learning to play an instrument or perfect a sport, the process is not instantaneous. If you were learning how to ski, you would fall down repeatedly until you slowly, very slowly, got a sense of it. The same thing is true in learning to meditate. You forget; you come back. You forget; you come back. And you keep doing that. The forgetting happens a little less frequently as you become more skilled, just as you fall down less often when you have been skiing for a while. But even

Olympic skiers still fall, and deeply realized meditators still forget. That is the characteristic of the mind we are training.

....

Doubt

Doubt—thinking that what we are doing is not right and is not working—is one of the most insidious difficulties we encounter because it is tricky to recognize. It is that little voice inside that says, "You're the only person who isn't doing it right," or, "This is the wrong practice [or teacher or retreat] for you. What are you doing here?" Doubt often has the effect of draining away our determination, our energy, and our faith. Doubt feels as if we have pulled the plug in our spiritual bath, and all our resolve has gone down the hole.

You may feel extreme discomfort during your early meditation days because meditation can highlight difficulties in your life—and such experiences often precipitate doubt. It is similar to washing filthy clothes and seeing all the dirt and scum come to the surface. When that happens, strong energies arise—anger, desire, the comparing mind. You feel as if you are experiencing the darkest part of yourself. It is easy to lose faith in the process because you feel that even as teachers and books are talking about the Buddha-nature and the possibility of liberation, you are further away from it than before you started meditating.

Down on the cushion. One leg up, other leg up, wrap the blanket around me.

Set the timer: 45:00, 44:59, 44:58. Okay it's working.

Close eyes; take a deep breath.

Rising, falling, rising, falling. Oh, I'm getting hungry; contraction; rumbling. What do I have to eat for breakfast? Oooh, I think I'll have one of the great vegan oatmeal chocolate chip muffins from Bread & Circus. Those are so scrumptious! The ones from Gwen and Deb's are really good too, but I really shouldn't be eating them because they aren't vegan and I'm trying to keep that commitment. I wish they would get some good vegan muffins. But maybe it's not too horrible to have one once in a while—nobody's perfect. I really like their raspberry mocha ones. Oh, wanting, thinking.

Rising, falling, rising. Oh, no! Here comes the leg pain! I hate that tension, burning, tightness.

Rising, falling. Oh, it's getting worse. Why do I have to sit through this pain? What good is it to torture myself? But I'm such a wimp. Why can't I just watch the sensations? It's just a little pain. I'll never be able to be a good meditator if I can't sit through some pain. This is nothing. What about all of those monks and nuns being tortured by the Chinese in Tibet? What if I get cancer or something horrible? How will I be able to practice then? I can't even sit through a little pain in my legs. Oh, it's getting worse. I hate this! — Cynthia, a student

This student was beset by wave after wave of doubt, which often assails us when we have a specific idea of how things—especially our practice—should be: It should be less difficult or we should be having a different kind of experience. Doubt is especially challenging because it creates all kinds of story lines that seduce us into thinking that the doubts are true—that we are inadequate, or the path is inadequate, or circumstances are too difficult, and it is just impossible.

As we shall see in chapter 4, doubt was a great difficulty

that assailed Siddhartha, the Buddha-to-be. As Siddhartha meditated under a tree, determined to become enlightened, Mara, the personification of all the hindrances, said to him, "Who do you think you are, sitting here, trying to become enlightened?" Siddhartha, unshaken, touched the earth and asked the earth to witness his clear intention, through his many lives, to purify himself and to become a *buddha* ("awakened one"). After this invocation, he continued practicing. He found, as we do, that one of the best antidotes to doubt is anchoring the mind through concentration and cultivating continuous mindfulness to the chosen object in meditation.

When we experience doubt, we can turn for guidance to the Buddha's criteria for determining what is true and what is not true about our thoughts. He asked, "Are our thoughts skillful? Do our thoughts bring happiness? Are they a contribution to our well-being?" In contrast, the doubting mind jumps here and there with a feeling of dis-ease and often ill will or aversion.

Sometimes it is also very helpful to talk to others, especially teachers, on this spiritual path. The value of such sharing was affirmed by the Buddha when he said to his attendant Ananda: "The *whole* of this path is associating with friends and people who are wise and steeped in this practice, who are free of delusion and ignorance."

If remorse for actions in the past causes doubt to arise, it is comforting to look at the story of Angulimara, a sadistic serial killer who went on vicious, murderous rampages in the Buddha's time. Wherever he went, wearing a garland made of the fingers of his victims, terrified people ran away and hid. One day after doing his alms round, the Buddha began to walk along a road to where Angulimara was lurking. Monks, herders, and farmers urgently warned him not to go ahead, but he ignored them and continued alone when they ran away. Angulimara, who was as well known for his fearlessness as for his cruelty, saw the Buddha coming and was quite perplexed by his calmness and lack of fear. Angulimara watched him pass, then stepped out onto the path to follow him. Although the Buddha appeared to be walking at a normal rate, Angulimara could not catch up with him, no matter how fast he walked. To find out who this robed stranger was, Angulimara called out, "Stop." The Buddha replied, "I have stopped, but you have not. I abstain from violence toward all beings, but you have no restraint toward anything that lives. That is why I say I have stopped and you have not." Angulimara was profoundly struck by the Buddha's words, threw away his weapons, and asked to be taken on as a disciple right then. The Buddha accepted him. For years afterward, people threw rocks and rotten food at Angulimara, but he understood that this was the natural consequence of his previous actions and accepted this treatment without reaction. Angulimara went on to practice diligently, even performing miracles such as healing a deformed infant, and he reached the stage of *arahant*, a being free of all impurities of the heart and mind. Whenever we feel the doubt of self-negation, we can remember the story of Angulimara. If such a being could be transformed, so can we.

The hindrances are expressions of our untrained minds. We never deserve judgment or criticism for experiencing them. In the same way that we bring forth infinite patience and perseverance in training our children or pets to know what is safe and what is not, the invitation in Insight Meditation is to call forth the same kind of patient effort for ourselves. We do not repress or reject the hindrances but rather cultivate a relationship to them with awareness, loving-kindness, and perseverance. Creating this right relationship is how transformation begins.

Exercise: The Hindrances

Explore each of the hindrances for a day or for a week.

- Notice your relationship to each one. Use any of the suggested antidotes, and observe what happens.
- Think through what your day would have been like if you had not thought that some of it should have been different (for example, "The boss should have been congratulating me instead of complaining about the mailroom"; "I wish I had Sensodyne toothpaste.").
- Keep a journal or take some moments before you fall asleep to reflect on your day and what you learned about the hindrances.
- Appreciate your efforts.

4. The 2,500-Year Journey

When I was twelve years old, my family moved from South Africa to London. Soon afterward, walking along on a gray drizzly day, I turned to my mother and asked: "What is the point of life, Mum? Why are we living?" It was a familiar question for me, resounding through my being from a very young age—though usually not as clearly as at that moment in a new and very alien place.

I think the question had haunted me ever since I had become very ill as a young child. During a polio epidemic in South Africa in 1955–56, I developed extremely infectious bulbar polio and was put into a hospital room alone. I became so sick, I nearly died. For weeks I never saw my parents or any family members because the doctors were isolating me. It was a profound experience to come so close to death in such a difficult way—alone, unable to move, unable to eat. Decades later, when I encountered the story of the Buddha's life, it resonated with my experience of polio and my questions about the meaning of being alive. — AW

When the young man who would become the historical Buddha for the first time encountered old age, illness, and death—encounters that shocked him—he realized that no one could escape them and that none of the pleasures of life had ultimate value because they *all* would end. He was overcome by a deep desire to find something that transcended this reality. The inspiration for his quest was not the dream of some kind of heavenly realm or the idea of making himself a better person but rather the need to find something that does not have to end in death. Because his search so clearly parallels our own experience as human beings, we will look at his life in some detail.

The Buddha's Life

About 2,500 years ago, Suddhodana, the ruler of the Sakya clan in present-day Nepal, consulted a soothsayer about the approaching birth of his child. The sage told Suddhodana that the child would be a son and would become either a great ruler or a great spiritual leader. Suddhodana very much wanted his son, named Siddhartha Gautama (in Sanskrit, the most commonly used form; in Pali, Siddhatta Gotama), to follow in his footsteps, so to entice Siddhartha to remain and inherit the kingdom, he consciously created an environment that was as close to paradise as possible. Siddhartha lived in different palaces according to the seasons of the year: When it was hot, the family moved higher up into the mountains. When it was cold, they moved lower again. At each residence,

Suddhodana had planted exquisite gardens, beautifully laid out with trees and pleasant views, exotic birds, ponds, lakes, and tinkling water. But these gardens were walled in, so that Siddhartha could not see beyond them.

Within the luxurious palaces, all the servants were at Siddhartha's call, and he could experience every delight possible: beautiful sights, delicious foods, and ravishing women. He was brave and became expert at martial arts. Extremely handsome, strong, lithe, and intelligent, he happened to be the ideal son.

Siddhartha was confined within this seemingly perfect environment, but he was not isolated. He had many friends and a close relationship with his cousins. When he was sixteen, he married Yasodhara, a beautiful, intelligent, and generous woman who was known as a spiritual person devoted to helping people less fortunate than herself. Yasodhara seemed the perfect life partner for Siddhartha, and according to some stories, she supported him in his early questions about life. Thirteen years later, she gave birth to their son, Rahula.

During his twenties, Siddhartha had four experiences during outings from the palace that changed his life and our history. One night while riding in his chariot, he saw, for the first time in his life—because the king had made sure that there was none inside the palace—someone who was old: gray hair, wrinkles, cataracts growing over the eyes, a bent body. When Siddhartha asked his charioteer what he was seeing, the man explained that this was old age and that all of us are heir to it. Imagine how startling it must be to encounter old age for the first time in your twenties and to learn that all human beings will come to this particular state, including you. On three subsequent trips, Siddhartha saw for the first time someone who was very sick, a corpse surrounded by mourners, and finally a spiritual seeker, a *sadhu*.

On each trip he asked his driver what he was seeing. Just as he had never seen someone who was very aged, neither had he seen debilitating illness, the grief of people who have lost a loved one, a dead body, or a wandering ascetic. Siddhartha's initial questions became increasingly deeper. What does it mean to become very old? To be sick? To die? Even to be born and live our lives as human beings? He felt a burning desire to find out why we live and if there is anything that transcends birth, sickness, old age, and death. He wanted to know whether the cycle of living—of eating, washing ourselves, working, loving in our relationships, getting sick, and dying—is *it*, or if there is something more. Seeing the *sadhu* let him know that others were also seeking answers to the questions that plagued him.

Like Siddhartha, we have the same questions: What is our life about? Why are we alive? What sense of dis-ease in our being keeps us seeking something but we do not know what?

When he was twenty-nine, soon after Rahula's birth, Siddhartha told his wife that he had an urgent longing to go on a spiritual quest. His desire was not unlike whatever inspired you to pick up this book—it was the same search for learning, for wanting to find answers to fundamental questions of life. There are various stories of Siddhartha's leavetaking—even that he sneaked out at night, though he once described his family's grief as they watched him leave.

Although it is not clear from the stories that have come down to us, Siddhartha's wife—a spiritual seeker in her own right—probably encouraged him with words such as "Go find out the answers for us. I'm here with your son, and I'm behind you in your quest. I do not think you can do anything more important." From what we know about Siddhartha's character, it is unlikely that he was being irresponsible or did not care about his wife or his family—some scholars have even specu-lated that he delayed beginning his search until he had a son who could inherit rule of the Sakya clan. To use a contempo-rary analogy, the situation was probably like that of a family caught in terrible snowstorm in which their car becomes stuck in a drift; the husband's only choice is to go out—to leave the wife and child in the car—to try to find help. Similarly, from the stories about Yasodhara and the karma that led her to be Siddhartha's wife, this probably was a communal decision in which she said to him, "Go, but come back." And he did.

The night Siddhartha left, he acted in a radical way that represents renunciation for us: He cut off his beautiful long black hair, took off his elegant garments, and put on a simple robe, letting go of his old way of being through these symbolic acts. For six years, he wandered as an ascetic in northern India in search of gurus, or spiritual teachers. He studied with several of the most noted and mastered a form of meditation called *concentration*, or, in the Pali language, *samadhi*. In *samadhi*, you keep your focus on one object, not letting your mind waver. Eventually, you become absorbed into a very deep state of bliss, then equanimity, then a spacious condition without any sense of subject-object, without any sense of dualism—with a deep experience of unity. But these blissful states did not last, so Siddhartha intensified his ascetic practices: He whipped his body, did not bathe, and ended up in a group with others who ate just one grain of rice a day. Siddhartha became weaker and weaker, yet he had still not found *it*—he had not found transcendence.

One day sitting by a river, emaciated and almost uncon-scious from weakness, Siddhartha realized that extreme self-mortification is not the way. He bathed, then sat to meditate under a tree, where a young woman offered him a bowl of milk out of compassion. He accepted. Five fellow ascetics who had been traveling with him believed that he was merely giving in to base desires, so they rejected him and left him.

After Siddhartha regained some of his strength, he knew that he was ready to make his last stand to find enlightenment. Near Bodhgaya, in northern India, he sat down to meditate and vowed not to get up until he found total freedom. He sat under a *bodhi* (fig) *tree*, watching his mind—some accounts say for one night, others for forty-nine. In the process of meditating, he was assailed, so the story goes, by the forces of *Mara*—by all the energies that beset us when we first sit down, which we examined in chapter 3. Siddhartha experienced restless mind, daydreams of beautiful women seducing him, and perhaps the doubtful thought "What am I doing here? Maybe I should go back to the palace and my wife."

Even as he was assailed by demonic energies, Siddhartha nevertheless realized that nothing was as important as his quest for freedom, so he remained committed to it. Unmoved by all the energies coming through his mind and his body, he continued to meditate. When his mind was full of doubt, he saw the doubt and let it go. When his mind lacked energy, he saw that and his mind came to balance. When his mindfulness was weak, he saw that, allowing concentration to intensify. He kept strengthening the skillful qualities of mind through a deep presence of awareness (bare attention) so that his mind came to powerful equipoise and all the skillful factors came into balance: mindfulness, investigation, effort or energy, rapture, concentration, calm, and equanimity.

Then Siddhartha's mind expanded into the most spacious opening that a human mind can achieve. In that opening he saw all his previous lives, and he observed in each life the conditions that gave rise to what happened in the next life. He saw clearly for the first time the relationship of cause and effect, or *karma*. After witnessing all his own lifetimes, he saw the endless lives and deaths of all beings, their cycles, and the dynamic of cause and effect that operate in their lives and throughout the whole universe.

Finally, his mind encompassed all that a human mind can envision, and he saw the path of freedom unfold before him. He saw that we can practice a path of transformation by cultivating skillful mental conditions that bring about skillful results. Although he saw much more, he spent the next forty-five years teaching specifically about the kinds of conditions we need to create in our lives to bring about freedom from suffering.

After Siddhartha awakened to everything one could possibly know and saw clearly the path that liberates us, he became known as the *Buddha* (literally "Awakened One" in Pali and Sanskrit). As he was walking toward Benares, he came upon the five ascetics with whom he had spent years practicing. At first they rejected him for not holding true to their old practices. But the Buddha's presence was so radiant, they were curious about his transformation. It had come about through his enlightenment and his understanding of the *Middle Way*, which is a path neither of self-indulgence, as he had followed in his father's palaces, nor of severe asceticism, which had destroyed his physical and mental strength.

The Buddha asked the ascetics to hear him out. There at the *Deer Park* in Benares, he shared the *Four Noble Truths* of the existence, cause, and ending of suffering, which we will look at more closely in chapter 5. (For the text, see chapter 13.) He described how life is full of challenges but that we suffer because of our *relationship* to these difficulties. He explained that suffering results from the nature of being attached—of being imprisoned by craving—or from the opposite, aversion—not wanting things to be as they are. Then he talked about the possibility of freeing ourselves. He did not describe liberation as a kind of Walt Disney fantasy of paradise. He did not say, "Listen, when you are free, lots of money comes to you," or "When you are free, you are not sick," or "When you are free, you will have all the sexual partners you want"—or whatever we might think freedom is, usually an abundance of sense pleasures. Rather, the Buddha said that we know freedom when our fires of craving and ignorance have been burned out. When clinging and the hindrances have been eroded through our practices of not feeding them and letting go, we encounter our fundamental nature of goodness.

Then the Buddha laid out the *Eightfold Path* to liberation (pages 81–82). These teachings were so profound that the five ascetics knelt in front of him and asked to be his disciples. That was the beginning of his Sangha, followers practicing this path of freedom. For the next forty-five years, the Buddha taught about suffering and the end of suffering across northern India. He is believed to have died in Kusinara, India, in 486 or 483 B.C.E., at the age of eighty, possibly of food poisoning.

For us, the importance of the Buddha is not just that he asked universal questions about the meaning of life but also that he found answers to them. Perhaps when we become chronically ill or old, perhaps when we lose a loved one or open to the suffering in the world, we begin to understand the impermanent nature of our lives. We are moved to ask, "Is there something else? Is there a different way I can live that will help me face these difficulties?" The challenges of old age, sickness, and death, of separation from those we love, and even of natural disasters that destroy everything we have worked for and loved can become "gifts." They take us to our heart, which wishes to hold all these experiences without drowning us in suffering. We ask ourselves if there is an answer to that yearning in our hearts for an ultimate refuge, for a peace and happiness that are not dependent on living forever or on the pleasures in our world.

One of the greatest blessings possible in our lives is to come to a spiritual practice that invites this kind of happiness. That path began with the Buddha's first teaching in Deer Park, and it has come to us through an unbroken line of followers who have carried it from India throughout Asia and Europe to America.

The Spread of Buddhism in Asia

The Buddha saw himself not as a deity but as a teacher. Throughout his discourses, he encouraged his disciples to take what they had learned from him out into the world. On his deathbed, he encouraged them to "strive on untiringly." And so they did, first throughout India, then in the *Southern Transmission* to Southeast Asia, and later, in the *Northern Transmission*, the spread of Mahayana Buddhism to China, Korea, Vietnam, Japan, and Tibet.

BUDDHISM IN INDIA

Within only a month of the Buddha's passing in the middle of the fifth century B.C.E., disputes about some of his teachings arose, and his senior disciple, Mahakashyapa, called together five hundred elder followers for what is known as the *First Council*. Here several disciples recited the Buddha's discourses and rules for the Sangha, and the gathering affirmed the basic

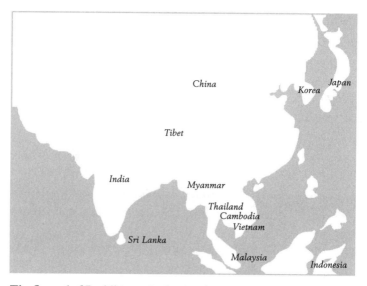

The Spread of Buddhism In the Southern Transmission, Buddhism spread from India to what is now Sri Lanka (Ceylon), Myanmar (Burma), Thailand, Kampuchea (Cambodia), and Indonesia. In the Northern Transmission, Buddhism spread into central Asia, China, Tibet, Korea, and Japan.

teachings that have come down to us as the foundation of the Theravada tradition.

Approximately a hundred years later, in the middle of the fourth century B.C.E., other disputes arose, particularly around whether monks could handle money. The *Second Council* was held to reaffirm the Buddha's teaching that they could not. After the Second Council, there was considerable fragmentation of the sangha, and one very strong group, the Mahasangha ("Great Sangha"), grew increasingly important. It was the forerunner of the Northern Transmission (see page 62) of *Mahayana* Buddhism, which includes *Zen* and *Tibetan* (*Vajrayana*) Buddhism.

The Third Council was called in the third century B.C.E. by Asoka, the Mauryan king of India. Asoka, a powerful ruler who united India through conquest, encountered a monk after a particularly bloody battle and had a battlefield conversion to Buddhism. Afterward, he declared India to be a Buddhist state, living under doctrines of peace and nonharming, and he was instrumental in the spread of Buddhism to Southeast Asia.

In about 100 C.E., King Kanisha called the Fourth Council to reaffirm the teachings. India was undergoing many changes, including the widespread use of written language—with the first written versions of the Dharma—and the further fragmentation of Buddhist sects.

For nearly a thousand years, the Buddha's teachings were spread throughout India, but by the thirteenth century they had been virtually eliminated in the country where they originated. Three major factors first weakened, then helped to dislodge Buddhism in India: the continuing fragmentation of Buddhist sects, the resurgence of native Hindu theistic traditions, and Buddhism's displacement by Islam, in teachings brought by Muslim conquerors. But in the areas of both the Southern and the Northern Transmissions, Buddhism continued to grow.

THE SOUTHERN TRANSMISSION

Buddhism may have been brought by traveling merchants to Southeast Asia as early as the Buddha's lifetime. It is certain that Asoka carried it there in the third century B.C.E., and it still flourishes in many areas of Southeast Asia today.

Our best indications are that over a period of centuries of interaction, Buddhism burgeoned in what are today major countries:

- *Burma* (Myanmar). Buddhism was found in Burma by the third century B.C.E. King Anaratha in the mid-eleventh century affirmed Theravada Buddhism as the Burmese state religion, as it is today.
- *Ceylon* (Sri Lanka). According to traditional stories, two children of King Asoka brought Buddhism from India to Ceylon in 250 B.C.E. Ceylon also had very early contact with Burma, and Buddhism has existed in various forms there ever since. In the twentieth century, Buddhism has been an influence in contemporary national movements.
- *Cambodia* (Kampuchea). Cambodia's involvement with Buddhism probably goes back to the third century C.E., and Theravada Buddhism has been dominant since at least the early fourteenth century.
- *Thailand*. King Asoka's missionaries may have carried Buddhism to Thailand from Burma in the third century B.C.E. In the nineteenth century it became the strong national religion it is today.
- *Indonesia*. Buddhism reached Indonesia much later and flowered there from the fifth through the fourteenth century. But by the early fifteenth century, it had been almost entirely displaced by Islam.

The history of Theravada Buddhism in Southeast Asia is especially important for those who practice Insight Meditation, because it was Southeast Asian teachers and their Western students who brought Theravada Buddhism to the West.

THE NORTHERN TRANSMISSION
Especially after the Second Council, Buddhism fragmented into a number of sects. In many parts of Asia, including Southeast Asia, the new sects coexisted—sometimes in the same monasteries—with Theravada Buddhism. During the North-

ern Transmission, Mahayana ("Greater Vehicle") emerged as the strongest of the new sects, and as it moved from country to country, it was deeply influenced by indigenous cultures:

- ○ *China.* In the first century C.E., various Buddhist sects arose in China, often introduced by merchants traveling along the Silk Route from central Asia. In China, Buddhism was influenced first by Taoism, then by Confucianism. The strongest sects have been *Ch'an* (Zen) and Pure Land, especially in Taiwan.
- ○ *Korea.* Buddhism was introduced into Korea from China in the fourth century C.E. Son, the Korean form of Ch'an, became dominant among the many sects that have existed and blended there.
- ○ *Vietnam.* Theravada Buddhism from India was an early presence in southern Vietnam, but after the sixth century, the Chinese influence was stronger. Of the various Buddhist traditions there, the strongest has been Thien, Vietnam's version of Ch'an.
- ○ *Japan.* Buddhism reached Japan from Korea in the mid-sixth century, and when Ch'an was brought from China in the late twelfth century, Zen became its most widespread tradition. In Japan, Zen absorbed many of the aesthetic qualities of Japanese culture, which have made it especially attractive in the West.
- ○ *Tibet.* Buddhism came to Tibet in waves, brought by noted Indian teachers beginning in the eighth century. Four major schools of *Vajrayana* ("Diamond Vehicle") Buddhism emerged in Tibet and spread into other Himalayan kingdoms and Mongolia. The popularity of the Dalai Lama and his receiving the Nobel Peace Prize have increased interest in Tibetan Buddhism in the West.

Buddhism Comes to the West

In the 1930s Buddhism was already familiar to many Westerners, especially European intellectuals, and many texts had
received excellent translations. In the United States its notable
growth in popularity began in the 1940s and 1950s with the
teachings and writings of D. T. Suzuki and was soon enhanced
by adherents such as Allen Ginsberg, Jack Kerouac, and the
other "Dharma bums." Buddhism took hold first through the
teachings of visiting Asian teachers, then through the involvement of Western teachers, and finally through the impact of
immigrant populations. In the process, Western Buddhism
acquired a distinct "personality" of its own.

Especially since Western teachers have become influential,
several major differences from Buddhism's Asian foundations
have emerged in Western Buddhism. First, Western Buddhism
is overwhelmingly lay rather than monastic in orientation, although monasteries have been established in all traditions. Second, Western women play major roles as teachers, unlike Asian
Buddhist women. Also, where Asian Buddhist traditions are relatively discrete, often because of geography, Western Buddhists
are much more ecumenical in their outlook and practice.

These three elements are manifested in the history of
Theravada Buddhism in the West. Many decades ago, Asian
Theravada meditation masters came to the West, especially
England, and a major Sri Lankan sangha was established in the
1960s in Washington, D.C. But only when Westerners who
had trained in Burma, Thailand, and India and their teachers
began to teach here did Theravada Buddhism—usually called
Vipassana or Insight Meditation—attract significant numbers
of Western adherents. Joseph Goldstein, Sharon Salzberg, Jack

Kornfield, and others established the Insight Meditation Society in Barre, Massachusetts, in 1975, for the first time giving lay-people in the United States the opportunity to strengthen their practice within a retreat setting. Many other Insight Meditation retreat centers, including Spirit Rock Meditation Center in Woodacre, California, also cofounded by Jack Kornfield, now make this experience possible for thousands of lay practitioners every year. In recent years, monasteries in the Asian tradition have also been established in California, West Virginia, and Vermont, as well as in England, enabling men and women to ordain and live as monastics.

Women have played a prominent role in the growth of Insight Meditation in the West. Ruth Denison was one of the first Western women to be fully recognized as a teacher in the lineage of Burmese master U Ba Khin. Denison is founder

Ruth Denison One of the first Western women authorized to teach by an Asian teacher, Denison gives a Dharma talk at Dhamma Dena Desert Vipassana Center, which she founded in Joshua Tree, California.

and resident teacher of Dhamma Dena Desert Vipassana Center in Joshua Tree, California. Christina Feldman began teaching in the 1970s and is now a guiding teacher at the Insight Meditation Society and founding teacher at Gaia House in Devon, England. And as mentioned above, Sharon Salzberg is a cofounder of the first Insight Meditation center in the United States.

Because of the cultural fit that Western teachers have given Insight Meditation, it is believed to be the fastest-growing tradition in the United States. Hundreds of new sitting groups and meditation centers have arisen in recent years. (Major centers are listed in chapter 15.) In fact, a number of Asian teachers, observing the major trends in Western Theravada Buddhism, are convinced that the role of the West will be to take Buddhism back to Asia and, through its emphases on lay participation, egalitarian roles for women, and ecumenism, to rejuvenate it.

5. The Buddha's Basic Teachings: The Four Noble Truths

I spent the first eleven years of my life in Johannesburg, South Africa, where my parents were active in the struggle against apartheid. When I was ten, both were arrested and imprisoned without any kind of judicial proceedings. My sisters and I did not know if we would ever see them again and were very frightened. My parents were eventually released but a little while later received a tip that they were going to be rearrested. It became clear that if they wanted to see us and live as a family, we would have to leave the country. And so we left quickly on exit permits, which meant we gave up all rights of citizenship and the choice to ever return. I felt torn apart, leaving my homeland. Grief flooded the years that followed. — AW

The Four Noble Truths confront the pervasiveness of suffering in our own and others' lives. We are sometimes touched by the immense pain of people living in prison, being tortured, or being persecuted. We see the ravages of war and of murder. We know the sorrow of children dying from malnutrition or lack of medical care. We know the pain of children taking up arms to kill, either in our own schools or in wars overseas. We live with the anguish of those who have been raped or abused. We lose those we love to disease or to prisons. Some of us live without good health. We may be constantly stressed by pressures. We lose jobs where we have worked for thirty years, or we cannot find any work. We find ourselves caught in the despair of depression or the isolation of loneliness. Some of us have even felt so far away from our hearts that we have attempted to take our own lives.

It is difficult to open our hearts to the suffering that life brings, and we often try to push it away, ignore it, or even deny it—a phenomenon that is dramatically illustrated when terminally ill people swear that they are getting better just before they die. Although acknowledging pain rather than denying it can offer us a path of healing and freedom, facing suffering is not easy—sometimes it is *very* difficult. But it is deeply liberating to face our situation and say, "This is painful. This is suffering. This is really hard and difficult. This is a true description of my life and what I see around me."

The First Noble Truth

The Buddha saw the painful realities in our lives and spoke about them in the *First Noble Truth*. He said that all human beings experience great pain, from old age, sickness, and death, from getting what we do not want, and from not getting what we do want. These changing conditions are called *dukkha*, a

The Buddha Teaching
Here the Buddha enumerates the Four Noble Truths in a posture that represents his teaching career.

Pali word usually translated as "suffering" or "dis-ease." Because of his understanding and compassion, the Buddha spent forty-five years after his enlightenment teaching "one thing only: *dukkha* and the end of *dukkha*."

THE FIVE AGGREGATES

Sometimes the *dukkha* in our lives is dramatically visible; at other times, it just nibbles away at us, unseen by others. The Buddha described a particularly subtle level of *dukkha* in terms of five components that constitute a human being, known as the five *aggregates* (*skandhas* in Sanskrit). They describe how our mind and body function from a perspective quite different from that of the West, which might describe anatomical and physiological components such as musculature, circulation, the sympathetic nervous system, and the lobes of the brain.

In contrast, the Buddha grouped the components into *form* (the body); *feeling* (the quality of pleasantness, unpleasantness, or neither—sometimes called neutral); *perception; mental formations* (thoughts, emotions such as love and anger, and mindfulness); and *consciousness*. This last component is quite different from our usual understanding of consciousness. When most people speak of higher consciousness, they are talking about qualities like wisdom and compassion. But the Buddha, through examining carefully his own processes, saw that consciousness arises when one of our senses makes contact with the outside world. So, for example, there is visual consciousness when the eye makes contact with a tree. When the ear first hears sound, there is auditory consciousness, and so on. In addition to sight, hearing, taste, touch, and smell, the Buddha included a sixth sense—the mind—in this group, so when the mind has a thought, there is mind consciousness.

The Buddha broke down our functioning into these five aggregates so we could see that the parts that make us up are constantly changing. Ordinarily we can easily see how our breath changes and how the sensations in our bodies keep changing. If we see ourselves as the five aggregates, it becomes easier to understand that everything that makes up "the one who perceives" is also changing.

Each of the aggregates is constantly arising and passing away, despite our feeling that there is a solid "I." Mindfulness helps us to see that both the perceiver *and* what is perceived are always changing. The "I" that is noticing an inconstant sensation, such as movement of the breath, is not a solid entity but, like the physical sensation, is changing. So perceptions, thoughts, feelings, and consciousness—all are arising and passing away continually, in an unceasing change that the Buddha also described as *dukkha*. As we deepen our meditation practice, we can see these elements that we call "I." As we see them changing over and over again, our identification with them—or the notion of "I"—falls away, and we open into a spaciousness that is free of all clinging and suffering.

FINDING BALANCE

Acknowledging suffering is not a linear process or a one-time opening. Rather, it is an ongoing path of achieving and maintaining balance. From time to time we may need to change how we are working with our difficulties. Sometimes finding the courage to open to difficulties that we have been avoiding is the right path. At other times, admitting what is painful can seem staggering, and we may need to back off. When we feel we are drowning in our own or others' pain, we can cultivate joy, appreciation, gratitude, or lovingkindness—energies that strengthen the mind and provide spaciousness so we can again hold what is difficult without reaction.

Having the flexibility to maintain balance enables us to live in the real world with an open heart. It takes time and a lot of trial and error to develop. The guidance of a teacher can be especially helpful as we try to learn when to make the great effort to face what is difficult and when to let go and rest.

When the Buddha talked about freedom in relationship to *dukkha*, he was not referring to a freedom that comes from blocking our hearts or shutting down. The Buddha's path, rather, is to reach out in sincere friendship to alleviate suffering *when we can*. Our hearts can expand in compassion and companionship to share and hold our own and others' suffering. At the same time, it is important to remain at peace when we are not able to reach out or to help. After you have been meditating for a while, you may feel you should be able to reach out to help others or to hold all your own difficulties with compassion instead of aversion or frustration. If you cannot, you may find yourself faced not only with difficulties but also now with negative self-judgment.

But Insight Meditation does not expect us to always be able to respond with open-hearted compassion. Sometimes we cannot, and that is the way it is. In such instances, we must be cautious not to add negative self-judgments. That phenomenon the Buddha compared to being struck by two arrows: Something happens to cause us pain, such as becoming ill, breaking up with a partner, or losing a job (the first arrow), then we heap self-blame on ourselves, shooting a second arrow right into the first wound. Insight Meditation is seeing ourselves as we are, without judgment.

The Second Noble Truth

After seeing the reality of the changing and difficult conditions of our lives, the Buddha was able to discern that the root cause of our suffering is attachment, or craving. This explanation of the cause of suffering is the *Second Noble Truth*. Whenever we desire or cling to or try to hold on to any experience, we are creating the condition for suffering. Again, this is a radical departure from what Westerners have been taught. Grasping for the ideal life partner or the ideal job, for success, money, or power is often considered not only the right thing to do but the best thing to do with our lives. What a huge turnaround it is to see this behavior in a more critical light!

The Buddha saw that the nature of the untrained mind is to crave pleasant experiences or to push unpleasant experiences away. He specifically outlined four areas of attachment that cause us greatest suffering: attachment to sensory pleasures, to opinions and beliefs, to rites and rituals, and to "I."

ATTACHMENT TO SENSORY PLEASURES

The desire for sensory pleasure is one of the primary forces in our lives. We live for pleasurable experiences—one after the other, and again one after the other. You can get a hint of your attachment to sensory pleasures by indulging in a brief fantasy of winning a lottery. What are the first things you think of that you would buy with the money? A new car. A vacation in the Caribbean. A new house with a swimming pool and a hot tub. A chef to create all your favorite dishes. A new wardrobe. A personal trainer. An orchestra to play your favorite music. A new library. Your fantasy would probably cover all the sense bases—beautiful sights, sounds, tastes, touch, smells, and thoughts.

As we noted in chapter 3, desire makes its object more attractive than it really is. When we feel desire, we project onto that object attractive qualities and become blind to its unattractive qualities. We have all experienced the sudden appearance of unattractive qualities once a desire has been fulfilled. For some of us it happens with chocolate cake. We are sitting at a restaurant after a good meal when the waiter walks past our table with desserts. On the platter is a piece of Black Forest cake. As we look at it, we imagine the taste—sweet and chocolate—and the smooth glide down our throat. Our mouth waters in anticipation, we think about the small buzz afterward, the chocolate's smell beckons to us—and we go for it. As we eat the cake, it is delicious. Afterward, we find ourselves feeling bloated and sick, and the chocolate keeps us awake most of the night. The reality is that even when the pleasures we get from sensory experiences are "perfect," they come to an end.

Another quality of desire is that it creates the illusion of permanence, the idea that *this* wonderful experience will make us happy and that that happiness will not change.

When I was a schoolgirl in London, the weather was interminably gray, buildings did not have modern heating, and our school uniform was a thin gray skirt, a white cotton shirt, and a small blazer—no coat or tights. I was freezing all the time, clenched in some contortion to keep myself warm. I spent hours dreaming about a wonderful vacation I had once had by the sunny Mediterranean in Italy. When I finally got to go there again, the reality was that the beaches were horribly overcrowded and were inhabited by sand fleas, and the sea was full of jellyfish. It was impossible to doze in the sun or hang out in the warm water without being bitten or stung. — AW

Because desire can never be satisfied, it is through desire that we are caught. No matter how wonderful the experience, it will come to an end, and then we will be faced with our desire once again. It is like heading home at the end of the day—hunched over the steering wheel, foot hard on the accelerator, driving as though the driving experience does not count—filled with desire to relax with a cup of tea or a drink and dinner. But who knows what is really going to happen once you arrive home? Twenty telephone messages with bad news might await you. But at the moment of rushing there, your mind moves into the future, into the idea of the next pleasurable experience, so that you are not actually connected with the experience in the present. What an awful way to live, excluding so much of our lives because we are caught up in an idea of what the future might bring us.

The Buddha asked us to notice the times when we are attached to pleasant sensory experiences and to notice the consequences of that attachment—to see whether that grasping actually serves our happiness. Have you ever noticed the contraction desire brings you, and also the feeling of separation? Have you noticed how easy it is to lose balance with desire, or when the desire becomes stronger and turns into craving, how you may find yourself a victim to the object you desire, clinging to it for your happiness? This is how we lose our capacity to remain whole and equanimous. Does desiring really serve your heart's vision?

ATTACHMENT TO OPINIONS AND BELIEFS

Just as we can become attached to things and people, so too we grasp our opinions as if they are perfect and will never change. Our attachment to opinions and beliefs is profound, in some ways more subtle and difficult to see than our attachment to sensual pleasures. The very nature of the attachment seems to give our opinions the light of veracity. We often feel justified, determined, even proud to hold on to ideas we feel are "true and right."

The destructiveness of holding on to unexamined ideas was brought home to me one day by a friend who told me this story: "When I was fourteen, I decided that I would never get married. I was one free guy and intended to stay that way. When I was twenty-two, I fell in love with this incredible young lady. And did she want to get married! She nagged me all the time for nearly twenty years, but I told her I was never going to get married. So she finally said, 'If you do not marry me by the time I'm forty, I'm going to leave you.' You know what I said. So she turned forty, and she left. And do you know what I am? I'm a lonely fifty-four-year-old man living with a fourteen-year-old's decision." — JS

The Buddha stressed that our attachment to opinions and beliefs can never bring happiness. Attachment divides and separates us. Have you ever found yourself not really listening to someone, even a dear friend, because you do not agree with her or him? Or relegating a whole group of people to "enemy" status because of differences of opinion? When this attachment is mixed with religion, the result can be deadly, as the history of Crusades, holy wars, and what has happened between Protestants and Catholics in Northern Ireland have shown. Even within Buddhism, we can become so attached to our own tradition—Insight Meditation, Zen, or Vajrayana, for example—that we put down "the others."

ATTACHMENT TO RITES AND RITUALS

When we look at what creates lasting transformation and what does not, the Buddha urged us to examine our attachment to rituals. Many Americans, as children, become so obsessed with the street rhyme "Step on a crack, break your mother's back" that even as adults they still avoid cracks in the sidewalk when they walk down the street. In the same rigid way, we may insist, for example, that we must sit in a particular meditation posture, say certain words, bow in a fixed manner, or go through a set of unchangeable meditation steps.

One New Year's Eve at Ruth Denison's retreat center, we were all dressed up, moving to the beat of a drum, circling around *each other. At one point we even had our sitting cushions on our heads. A new student opened the door and came into the meditation hall. Her mouth dropped open. One could see her disbelief. This could not be meditation! But it was: We were cultivating mindfulness and joy.* — AW

Are we so attached to our habitual ways of doing things that they have become the *only* way to do them? If a friend takes you somewhere by a different route from the one you usually take, do you experience a flash of discomfort because "your" way feels like the right way? In even the smallest details of our lives, we can overemphasize form and forget that it is the skillful qualities of mind that will transform our heart.

ATTACHMENT TO "I"

The section on the First Noble Truth introduced the five aggregates. We meet them again in this section. Our attachment to "I" is probably the most difficult to untangle. We have a sure and certain sense of ourselves as "here," as "I did," and as "this is me," but this sense of "I" comes about only through attachment. If we investigate ourselves very carefully, we find thoughts, physical sensations, and feelings of unpleasantness, pleasantness, or neither pleasant nor unpleasant. We find different feelings of joy, love, anger, faith, and envy. We find perception and memory. All of these experiences do not stay the same; even our thoughts of ourselves do not stay the same. So where is the solid "I"? A frequently used metaphor is that of the rainbow: When the right combination of temperature, moisture, and light occurs, we say that there is a rainbow, though no permanent, unchanging *thing* that is a rainbow exists. In the same way, when the right combination of aggregates occurs, we say that a particular child exists. But if this child were a permanent, unchanging being, she would never grow up to be an adult.

Imagine the wonderful freedom that comes from beginning to have some distance from our "I am this" or "that." If we have no attachment to ourselves, we have no need to defend ourselves. We can live with an open heart and mind. If we have no attachment, we have no need to hoard, lie, or hurt others. We do not need to play out roles that we think we should play as teachers, students, or parents. Rather, we can live as ourselves and as teachers, students, or parents with ease and well-being. Our greatest contraction and isolation are linked to our ownership of and belief in a permanent "I" and the consequent organization of all experiences around it.

The Third Noble Truth

The *Third Noble Truth* tells us that an end to suffering is possible: Each moment in which there is no attachment is a moment free of suffering. At such times we experience the spaciousness of having no separate self and a profound connection with all of life. We may have already experienced these moments and called them sacred or special. The Third Noble Truth acknowledges these experiences and invites us to live our whole lives in this manner.

The Buddha's path builds our capacity to live without clinging and can bring us to what is called the unconditioned, or *Nirvana* (Sanskrit; *Nibbana* in Pali). Nirvana is also called the Unborn, the Unoriginated, the Uncreated, or the Unformed because it is outside our usual experiences. It is not called an experience because it does not come into being and then fall away as our other daily experiences do.

Opening to the unconditioned is considered the highest peace. The unconditioned brings with it unshakable insight into the absence of self, and through successive openings all remaining obstacles to our freedom are purified. With the fading away of all clinging, there comes the extinction of suffering. Our experience of the unconditioned can change us permanently, so that we cannot go back into all of the old habit patterns that did not serve us.

Our capacity to open to unconditional happiness and freedom, which we considered in relationship to the First Refuge (pages 6–7), also underlies the Third Noble Truth. We can consider the unconditioned as our fundamental nature of freedom. It is described as illuminated and unobstructed openness, as awareness that has no boundaries and pervades space, as an emptiness that is so wide that it can hold absolutely everything without any grasping or attachment. An apt metaphor for the spaciousness of our essential nature would be what happens if you pour a cup of salt into the ocean: The ocean is so immense that the cup of salt will not have any impact on its nature. Or imagine sitting at the top of a high mountain and seeing for hundreds of miles around you the peaks of other mountains and the endless blue sky. The silence surrounding you is pierced by the cry of a hawk, but the sound dies away without changing the spaciousness around you.

This unbounded awareness is the expression of unlimited *compassion* and love—qualities reflected in the great teachers mentioned in chapter 1. The story of Jesus on the cross begging God to forgive those who were crucifying him is a beautiful example of a love that is always there, no matter what is happening. Our fundamental nature has absolute ease of being and peace. It touches and is touched by everything, without an agenda, reaction, or opinion. It does not exist on the level of conceptual thought, in stories and opinions. The good news is that we *can* uncover it through our practice, though we often encounter doubt as we seek it.

Once a student approached the contemporary Indian teacher Poonjaji and said, "I really want to free myself from suffering." Poonjaji replied, "Do you want it enough? Enough to really free yourself?" When I heard the student questioning Poonjaji, I saw the doubt lying within me: I believed I could not discover freedom. Then the question arose "Why do I hold on to an idea that serves no purpose other than keeping me imprisoned? Why not let go now?" — AW

Each moment we live without clinging or aversion, we live in freedom, and these moments continue to build on one another. Although people uncover their fundamental nature in different ways, all who are fully awakened share the common quality of having no clinging, no greed, no hatred, and no delusion.

Uncovering our essential nature does not mean we will not experience pain. Our bodies in their very constitution have the capacity to experience pain, and they will do so as we grow older or get sick. It does not mean we will not feel sad or tired. What it means is that we are awake—we know where we are and we are present with our experience, with what life brings, without judgment or reaction or clinging. In a well-known story, the Buddha encountered curious passersby who, impressed by his startling presence, asked him if he was a king or a god. When he said no, they challenged him by saying, "Then what are you?" He quietly responded, "I am awake."

The Fourth Noble Truth:
The Noble Eightfold Path

The *Fourth Noble Truth*, the *Eightfold Path*, is a detailed map addressing the other three Noble Truths, laying out precisely how to end suffering. Traditional teachings start with Right View (or Right Understanding) and Right Intention (or Right Thought)—seen as the category of *wisdom*, discussed in detail in chapter 6. The second category, *morality* (chapter 7), comprises Right Speech, Right Action, and Right Livelihood. The third category, *concentration* (chapter 8), includes Right Effort, Right Mindfulness, and Right Concentration. The Eightfold Path is not linear; all its parts are interconnected. Each link on the path supports and is dependent on the others. Here we will look at a summary of the Eightfold Path, then in the three chapters that follow, we will look closely at the constituent parts.

- *Right View:* A thorough understanding of the Four Noble Truths—the truth of suffering, the origin of suffering, the cessation of suffering, and the Eightfold Path leading to the end of suffering. Understanding karma and dependent origination.
- *Right Intention:* Renouncing thoughts of ill will and cultivating skillful intentions.
- *Right Speech:* Abstaining from lying and determining whether the time for speech is appropriate and whether it is both useful and truthful; speaking in a way that causes no harm.
- *Right Action:* Living according to the Five Precepts—refraining from taking life, refraining from taking what is

not given, refraining from false speech, refraining from sexual misconduct, and refraining from taking intoxicants.

- ○ *Right Livelihood:* Supporting ourselves through work that is legal and peaceful and entails no harm to others—specifically, work that does not involve trading in arms or lethal weapons, intoxicants, or poisons, or killing animals.
- ○ *Right Effort:* Striving to awaken and strengthen skillful mental states and to renounce unskillful ones.
- ○ *Right Mindfulness:* Cultivating mindfulness of body, feelings, mind factors, and mind objects (*mind objects* means the essential teachings of the Buddha, or the Dharma; see chapter 5).
- ○ *Right Concentration:* Developing one-pointedness and skillful absorption for insight.

The Eightfold Path is a list not of rules but rather of invitations to live in a way that creates the conditions for opening and transformation. We enter not into an authoritarian or theological teaching, but into a process of seeing. For example, the invitation to refrain from taking life cannot be a blanket statement, because we take life all the time: We eat food—we eat vegetables if we are vegetarian; animals give their lives to us if we are not. What does nonharming mean then? If our kitchen is overrun with ants and cockroaches, is it Right Action to kill them? What if that kitchen is in a public restaurant? The difference in coming to decisions as part of our practice is that we do it with awareness and understanding—we comprehend what we are doing. And we can do it with a heart filled with kindness. The Dalai Lama has said that his most sacred spiritual practice is cultivating kindness and refraining from harming.

Exercise: Investigating Suffering

Take a little time to contemplate the experience of suffering in your life. Choose one painful incident in particular and either write or think about it.

Can you locate the underlying energies of wanting the experience to be different? Can you see the energy of desire or craving that the Buddha spoke about in the Second Noble Truth?

Can you contemplate another way of holding the experience that includes letting go of this desire or clinging?

What does freedom or enlightenment mean to you? Do you think you have the capacity to find freedom? If your answer is no, why not? Could you reframe your definition of *freedom* to give yourself this possibility? If so, how can you nurture this possibility?

6. The Eightfold Path: Wisdom

Some years ago it was common to hear the expression "That is your karma." I knew this phrase before I came to the Dharma, and I had tremendous difficulty with it because I thought teachers were saying that all those who suffer deserve to. I understood karma as some kind of fate or divine ruling: "You are bad, so this is what you get." I felt very defiant about karma. How could all beings who are suffering merit it? No one deserves suffering. After many years—and with a better understanding of karma—I can see that Buddhist practice does cherish the sacredness of all human beings by believing in our capacity to open our hearts and minds and purify our intentions and actions (karma). — AW

As we begin to understand suffering (the First Noble Truth) and the clinging that gives rise to it (the Second Noble Truth), we enter into the field of karma (pages 85–88), which describes the dynamic of the relationship between our intentions and their consequences on both a universal and a personal level. Looking closely, we can see how dependent origination (see pages 88–96) describes the moment-to-moment development of clinging and how it becomes solidified into the feeling of "I." As we deepen in our practice, we see for ourselves, over and over again, the truth of these dynamics, and in the seeing we are freed. In this first chapter on the Fourth Noble Truth, we begin by looking in detail at Right View and Right Intention, the first two links of the Eightfold Path, which explain the Buddha's teachings on wisdom.

....

Right View

Right View (or Right Understanding), is both the beginning and the culmination of the Eightfold Path. Right View orients us, giving us a framework and perspective to comprehend our lives. It includes understanding the Four Noble Truths, karma, and dependent origination, three intimately linked areas of understanding. Finally, it points out the direction that our efforts need to take and the transformation that is possible.

KARMA

The Buddha said that each moment of our lives is not determined by bad luck or chance. Rather, it is a consequence of our previous thoughts, actions, and spoken words. *What is going on in our lives is decided by an unbreakable relationship between our actions and the consequences of those actions.*

Karma—*volitional* action that wills and organizes the mind and body toward a goal—is a fundamental part of the Buddha's teaching. The volitional aspect of karma is critical. If, for example, you unknowingly step on an ant as you pass through your front door, the act does not bring future consequences because it was not volitional, or intended. In volitional actions and their results, what is important to discern is their ethical quality. If we are guided by generosity, ethics, and wisdom, then the results will support our freedom and happiness. But if our actions, speech, and thoughts are determined by greed, ill will, and delusion, then we will continue to intensify the suffering in our lives.

Vietnamese monk and meditation teacher Thich Nhat Hanh sometimes uses the analogy of the mind as a storehouse. In our storehouse we have many different seeds—seeds of love, mindfulness, concentration, energy, hatred, and delusion, all fifty-two of the qualities of mind. Whichever seeds we water will blossom and grow into plants. If we repeatedly act out of anger, we are watering the seeds of anger and will have a huge, blooming angry plant. The same is true for kindness. If we consistently meet our angry plant with kindness, the angry plant has nothing to nourish it and begins to wither and die, and the loving plant begins to thrive.

Just as real seeds need particular conditions in which to germinate and ripen—temperature, nutrients in the soil, and water—so does karma: The results of our actions depend on certain conditions for fruition, and we cannot foresee when these conditions will take place. Sometimes the results are immediate. For example, if we share our lunch with a friend, we might experience appreciation. If we have a surge of anger and act on it, we might feel heat, energy, and contraction. We may also immediately experience someone's response of anger toward us. But we may also encounter the results of these actions at another time in our lives or, as the Buddha said, in another lifetime. In the analogy of seeds, redwood tree seeds require intense heat to crack open and start rooting; the seeds may lie dormant for hundreds of years until a forest fire brings the necessary heat. This kind of dormancy may also exist for some of our own "seeds." So the results of our actions may depend on certain conditions coming into existence.

Another important characteristic of karma is that at each moment, as we experience the consequences of our past actions, we have the opportunity for input in the present. We have free will. *Mindfulness is so critical because by cultivating this skillful quality of mind, we see the places where we have choice.* If we are able to see how we are building our anger, for example, and see the suffering in it, we can make a choice to let it go. We can begin to change what arises for us in the future. We cannot build happiness unless we are present to meet what is arising with qualities such as kindness and generosity. Such qualities build a force in our future for their fruition—for more kindness, more generosity.

Karma has nothing to do with judging or condemning ourselves or others who face suffering. Rather, as has been a theme in this book, when we recognize pain, we open our hearts to meet it with love, and we try to alleviate suffering wherever we find it. Nothing in our experience or the experience of others deserves our judgment. Karma is not about "deserving" but about understanding what brings suffering into our lives and what reduces it.

Understanding karma can become our strongest inspiration for continuing to practice Insight Meditation.

A friend who read an early draft of this book mentioned that many of my stories about myself were negative. I wondered if I should change them, but I decided not to, because I want to share what I was like when I began this practice—probably not very different from many other beginners. Now, more than twenty years later, I live with so much more wisdom, love, generosity, faith, and open-heartedness. I live with much more ease and sense of well-being. This transformation has come about because of karma. — AW

Each moment of mindfulness builds awareness and effort. When we are caught in one of the hindrances, mindfulness inspires us to let go because we know, as Ruth Denison says, "Darling, karma means you can't get away with nothin'." And if we cannot let go of a hindrance in the moment, we can take refuge in our intention to let go of it in the future. Karma is our greatest source of empowerment because it inspires us to call forth the best of ourselves—wishes for love, compassion, patience, and gentleness. We always have this capacity to transform ourselves and our future.

What has brought me through difficult times? It is faith in the dynamic of karma. I know my best intentions are to refrain from harming and to open my heart to life. When I am really contracted, when I feel lost or unable to be mindful or loving, I keep in the back of my mind these intentions, and even if I don't feel them in the moment of being lost, I know they will carry me through difficult times. I also know that if I can hold the difficulties—or at least refrain from making them worse—my restraint is healing my future. — AW

DEPENDENT ORIGINATION

What inspires our actions? Why do we act the way we do? The Buddha described in twelve steps how our actions come into being and how they can build either our suffering or our happiness. To arise, each of these twelve steps is dependent on the particular conditions of the other steps, and the cycle is called *dependent origination*. The Buddha's explanation of how we work is complex and may be totally new to you, so take your time with it. You may want to read it several times.

Let us begin with the key concept of ignorance. The stories, habit patterns, and other unexamined opinions we have inherited from our past influence the way we experience ourselves and the world we live in. They influence how we see, hear, taste, smell, and experience touch and thoughts. Imagine yourself rowing on a river at sunset. The noises of the afternoon have quieted down, the sky is a light show of magnificent reds and oranges, and you feel a sense of peace growing inside. Suddenly your boat is jolted. You turn around, startled, and see that it has been hit by a boat with a woman in it. Furious, you bluster, "What the dickens are you doing? Why don't you look where you're going?" You grab your oars in anger and start rowing.

Now imagine the same scenario, but when you turn to look at what has jolted you, you see an empty boat. You guess that the boat must have come loose from its mooring and that the current must have carried it toward you. You feel no anger. What is the difference in your responses to the two situations? In the first incident, were you holding an opinion or building a story about how you think someone ought to behave in a boat? Did this story justify your anger? In the second incident, you had no reaction. You might accept a boat drifting in the water as part of the flow of what happens with the force of tides and experience the collision as just part of life. You have no irritation toward it.

These two stories illustrate how we project interpretations

onto our experiences. When we are subject to such interpretations, we lose the freedom the Buddha described when he said that in the seeing is only the seen, in the hearing only the heard, in the smelling only the smell, in the touching only the touch, in the thinking only the thought. Understanding the first step in this cycle of how we create our world invites us to investigate all the unexamined stories and habit patterns we carry, which influence how we see the world. The Buddha called these stories ignorance.

When we are unable to see—when we are ignorant of—what we are doing, we keep repeating the cycle of distorted perceptions, actions, and beliefs. The Buddha called this endless loop *samsara* (Sanskrit for "cycles of existence"). It is as though we were living in a dream where one cycle follows another without our actually knowing what is going on.

Let us now look at the twelve links of dependent origination that the Buddha outlined to describe *samsara*. An investigation into the links of dependent origination traditionally begins with ignorance, but it does not have to. It can begin anywhere in the cycle. The sequence of steps can be described in two ways, either through three life spans or in the moment-to-moment interaction in our lives.

Here is the cycle described in brief:

- *Ignorance.*
- *Karmic formations,* or all our volitional actions, thoughts, and words, depend upon the conditions of ignorance (of the Four Noble Truths).
- *Consciousness* depends upon the condition of karmic formations.
- *Mental and physical existence* depends upon the condition of consciousness.

- *The six sense organs* depend on mental and physical existence.
- *Contact, or sense impression,* depends on the six sense organs.
- *Feeling* (of pleasantness, unpleasantness, or neither pleasant nor unpleasant) depends on contact.
- *Craving* depends on feeling (the Second Noble Truth).
- *Clinging* depends on craving.
- *Becoming* depends on clinging.
- *Birth* depends on becoming.
- *Death* depends on birth.

Let us create another scenario to clarify these links. James is just starting a market-research business, but he feels a little insecure about how successful he will be. James's desire for success in this business is not just about making money; it is also about his sense of self-worth, for he has struggled a lot, especially with his parents and siblings, to prove he is "okay."

James is walking down Main Street, thinking about his new business, and he is caught in the unconscious desire "to be someone." His shoulders are a little tight, his chin juts forward, and his jaws are clenched. As he passes a Mazda car dealership, he sees his neighbor Richard staring at a new-model sports car. The car is sleek, and the red metal gleams brilliantly in the morning light. Its hood is open, and the engine proclaims power to all who pass by. Richard greets James, then turns and walks away, disgustedly remembering how a hotshot in a car just like this one ran a red light yesterday and almost caused an accident. But James stops, lingering in pleasure at what he sees. This car is a beauty. As he stands in front of it, desire takes hold of him. He wants this car. The longer he stands there, the stronger the desire becomes. His initial arguments to himself about not having enough money to pay for the car fall away. He feels he must have it. He walks through the doors of the showroom and finds a salesperson. As he test-drives the car, he knows this car is *him*. He feels important. The car is thrilling to drive and gives him pleasure. He buys the car, and the next day he drives it to his parents' home to show it off.

Three months later, as James is rushing to an appointment, anxious to make a good impression on a prospective client, he opens his car door, jumps in, and turns the key, impatient to get going. He stops for a red light, and while waiting he realizes he is already taking the car for granted—it really has not made much difference in how happy he is.

Let us reexamine this story in terms of the links of the dependent origination cycle. We start with *ignorance*—the stories, habit patterns, and other unexamined opinions we have inherited from our past that influence the way we experience the world and ourselves. They affect how we see, hear, taste, smell, and experience touch and thoughts. James is not aware of how his thoughts, feelings, and need to prove himself have been powerful forces in his life and a screen through which he has interpreted the world around him. He is not aware of how his desire "to make something" of himself is based on his assumption that he is not good enough. This necessity to become somebody has closed his capacity to see that his deepest empowerment would come from cultivating awareness and lovingkindness, not from getting something.

Ignorance could be defined as not understanding what causes our suffering and the ways to end it. We may devote ourselves to armoring ourselves against life and the world, to collecting things, or to becoming rich and famous—all in the conviction that these actions will bring about lasting happiness. We may believe that the beauty of our bodies will fulfill our lives. None of these things is bad or wrong in itself, but they all compel us to act out of a collection of accumulated beliefs rather than out of an understanding of what is true. When James first looked at the sports car, he did not see the color just as color and the shape of the car as its particular shape. What he saw was influenced by ignorance—the story of not being good enough and needing something more in order to feel good about himself.

With these unexamined beliefs and stories as a condition, *karmic formations* arise. Karmic formation is the movement of our unconscious ideas and beliefs into our intention to manifest them. It includes the energies we direct toward achieving the goals held in the stories we carry. In James's scenario, karmic formation is the movement of his intention to become "somebody" through his new business venture.

The first nonspecific impression of our world is called *consciousness*, which depends on karmic formations as a condition. Consciousness becomes the next step in the expression of our intentions, manifesting as a general awareness of sensations that enter through one of our senses. James is aware in a very general way of the cars going by on the street, other pedestrians on the sidewalk, and the automobile dealership he is passing, without noticing anything specifically. Consciousness comprises visual, auditory, taste, smell, and mind consciousness, but one sense consciousness predominates at any given time. These general impressions of consciousness become the condition for becoming more involved and solidified in the world through our *mental and physical existence*. James's mind and body are the expression of the willing of karmic formations and consciousness toward his goal of becoming someone special. His body and mind disclose this in how his body is walking—his hunched shoulders and clenched jaw—and in how his perceptions and memories come into being and are directed.

Mind and body become the condition for the *six sense organs* to manifest. We now interact with the world through the sense organs. James notices the car dealership through the general impression of visual consciousness, and his eyes are awakened.

Once his eyes have been awakened, *contact* takes place. James notices the details of the Mazda, its red gleaming metal shining through the window. Contact could also be auditory (between our ears and sound) or olfactory (between our tongue and food) or touch (through our body and whatever is touching it). Thought is also the object of the sense base mind.

With contact comes *feeling.* In these teachings *feeling* does not mean emotion but rather the experience of pleasantness, unpleasantness, or neither pleasant nor unpleasant. Every moment when one of our senses has contact, pleasant, unpleasant, or neither pleasant nor unpleasant feelings arise. When James sees the red sports car, pleasant sensations occur. It feels good to him just to stand there and look at it.

When we experience pleasure, our habitual response is to desire more pleasure. As James feels pleasure at seeing the sports car, desire arises; he wants it. This wanting is called *craving.*

With craving as a condition, *clinging* can arise. James might have stopped in front of the dealership, experienced the desire and even the craving to purchase the car, but contemplated his finances and continued to walk past. Clinging is not walking away but going with the craving. James walks into the dealership with clinging for the car.

Clinging brings the conditions for what is called *becoming.* When James drives the car, he is thrilled and feels he has become the somebody he had wanted to be. He feels special because he is now driving this dashing red sports car.

With becoming as a condition, *birth* arises. James buys the car and feels he has created—or we could say "birthed"—the person he really wants to be, proving to everyone that he is worthy of respect and love.

With birth as a condition, *death* arises. The term *death* describes the passing away of experiences. Three months later, James notices he no longer has the same feelings about the car. As he sits at the red light and notices the changes in his feelings, he feels the beginning of a whole new cycle, now in relation to the new client.

It is exciting to be able to trace the sequence of events in our experiences and to begin to demystify how the solid sense of identity arises. The Buddha's teachings on dependent origination describe the interconnection of all life and how each moment of experience has arisen from particular conditions. When we bring understanding to what is happening *in the very moment,* we can interrupt the cycles. We can explore how our thoughts and opinions determine how we interact in the world—why Richard walked away but James went into the showroom. We can investigate how they affect our perceptions. Are we really seeing what we are seeing, or are we superimposing, as James did, our ideas and desires so that our perceptions become distorted? Are we aware of the experience of pleasantness or unpleasantness and how our habitual mind moves into craving, as James's did, or aversion, as Richard's did? It is remarkable to see how many stories we build up in our lives around the experience of pleasantness or unpleasantness. What happens when we become one with these stories? Do we feel righteous? Do we feel relaxed, free?

Understanding dependent origination provides a framework within which we can understand our momentary experiences and the unconscious repetition of events that builds clinging into the prison of "I." The other links on the Eightfold Path provide detailed practices that give us the tools to challenge this cycle and transform it.

Right Intention

Understanding karma and dependent origination is an integral part of Right View and lays the foundation for Right Intention (also called Right Thought). Right Intention, in turn, gives rise to Right Speech, Action, and Livelihood, the next links in the Eightfold Path (chapter 7). As we come to understand the influence that our beliefs have in determining the amount of suffering we experience, we become interested in examining our thoughts. Throughout this book we have spoken of the vision we carry in our hearts for freedom, for a kind of well-being that comes from an unshakable inner peace. This vision is activated and is given a path by Right Intention. This path has three major components. The first is becoming aware of our thinking process; the second is renouncing old negative patterns; the third is cultivating goodwill.

As we begin to investigate our thoughts, we can ask ourselves, "Are these thoughts of benefit to myself and others? Do they come from kindness rather than desire?" In the story of the red sports car, James's thoughts of buying the car became a powerful force because he had no awareness of them. Are your thoughts actually in your heart's service?

Thinking, like desire, often seduces us into believing that if we just think some more, we will solve our problems. We find ourselves thinking about the future as though the act of thinking could somehow control events and make things happen. We find ourselves caught up in thinking of the past, as though this too would somehow put to right what has already happened. Wisdom is not the culmination of our thoughts. If it were, because we spend so much time living in our thoughts, we would all be so wise we would not need a spiritual practice. But wisdom is an expression of mindfulness, and mindfulness is not a thought. If we want to become clear about a particular problem or resolve a difficulty, the most effective strategy is to drop down from our habitual thoughts and practice mindfulness. Mindfulness, as we have said, has the capacity to *see clearly*, and clarity is what we want. It is possible to become mindful of our thinking process, but such awareness is difficult in the beginning because our thoughts can seduce us into their story line and we lose mindfulness to them.

In the second step, Right Intention does not ask us to *stop* thinking but rather to *renounce* thinking when it is habitual and not appropriate. Because the experience of living with our uncontrolled thinking process is so uncomfortable, when we come to a spiritual practice we feel sure that what we need to do is get rid of all our thoughts. Right Intention is not about getting rid of all our thoughts but about letting go of the thoughts that do not support our happiness and reduce our suffering. Many of our thoughts are a response to feelings of pleasantness, unpleasantness, or neither pleasant nor unpleasant, which arise (as we saw in our examination of dependent origination) each time one of our senses has contact with an object—for example, our eyes and a visual object. Often, as soon as we experience one of these feelings, our thoughts take off.

I recently was walking by the bay near Point Reyes, California. The view was extraordinarily beautiful, with hills covered by dark green trees, offsetting the blueness of the still water. I felt very contented. Without my realizing it, desire came up, with thoughts of how to increase this pleasure. How could I persuade my partner to move here? Where would we live? How far away is the airport so that I could travel to all my teaching commitments? I was so immersed in my thoughts that I no longer even saw the scenery that had evoked them. As soon as I caught myself thinking, I came back to walking in the beauty of the environment. — AW

We can spend hours in our thoughts because we want pleasant experiences or less unpleasant ones. Ironically, our thoughts take us away from the real pleasure in the moment. See if it is possible to catch yourself in one of these cycles of thinking. When you are walking or driving and find yourself lost in thinking, trying to solve some problem, see if you can come back to walking or driving. Returning to the body is a safe refuge. After letting go of your thoughts, notice what you are doing: sitting, holding the steering wheel, pressing on the accelerator, feeling that pressure there. Or become aware of the movement in the body that arises from walking. See if you can stay present with your experiences by noticing what is happening in your body.

Renunciation is an effective way to break the "top ten tapes" we play in our heads over and over again. We know most of our thoughts well because we have thought the same thoughts repeatedly. Have you noticed that after a while they do not contribute anything to your understanding or well-being? When was the last time you had an original thought? It is a wonderful practice to renounce a thought after having it more than two or three times.

Sometimes it is harder to renounce repetitive thoughts than at other times, especially if we have not looked at the underlying emotions associated with them (as mentioned in chapter 3). Before we can let go of a thought, we may have to acknowledge complex feelings below the surface, so it is valuable to take the time for an open-hearted investigation.

Some habitual thought patterns are so strong that renouncing them requires the energy of a spiritual warrior. We can call on this energy just as the Buddha called on the earth as his witness when he was sitting under the bodhi tree (page 56). We can even say out loud, "No! No! I will not go with you. I call on all my powers of strength, love, and wisdom to resist this thought." Some of our negative thought patterns have been repeated so often they "feel true." It is their familiarity that creates this illusion. *There are absolutely no negative thought patterns that are true.* One of the greatest gifts we can give ourselves is to renounce negative patterns of thought.

In the third aspect of Right Intention, we can cultivate joy, appreciation, and gratitude by praying, singing, blessing, and practicing the divine abodes (chapter 9). A powerful practice is to think of all the blessings we experience every day and/or to appreciate qualities of those we work with or love.

It is also helpful to make room in our lives to contemplate the challenges we face, the teachings, and our practice. Contemplation gives us the space for appropriate thinking and allows us to drop underneath the pattern of habitual thoughts and to see with awareness what is calling us. We can sit and first connect with our breathing, then open ourselves to "hold" a question in the quiet space of our nonthinking mind. Sitting with the question and presence of mind without "thinking" can create the space for new and creative solutions.

Exercise: Right Intention

Begin to notice your thoughts, and for one week keep a journal of the kinds of thoughts that predominate. Notice the qualities associated with your thoughts. Do they bring a sense of well-being? Of tension, anger, doubt, desire, contraction, or opening? Do they bring you into connection with life, or do they separate you further into the little box from which you are already struggling to free yourself?

Notice any physical qualities associated with your thoughts. Can you feel contraction, tension, and pressure associated with some thoughts, and openness, fluidity, and spaciousness with others?

See if you would like to let go of unskillful thoughts and cultivate skillful ones in one particular area of your life. Write down the kinds of thoughts you would like to cultivate and the ones you would like to let go of. For a week keep reminding yourself of this intention. Discern how the qualities associated with your thoughts tell you whether they fall into the category of Right Intention.

7. The Eightfold Path: Morality

When I was seven years old, I went with my mother to the local haberdashery, which had needles and fabrics. Lying by itself on a counter near the door was a glittery pink necklace. While my mother was talking with the salesperson, I was so enticed by the necklace that I put it in my pocket. The gesture felt daring and secretive. But when I got home, I realized I could never wear the necklace, because my parents would immediately ask where I had gotten it. I could not do anything with it, so I ended up throwing it into the garbage. This was a profound experience because even in the moment of being seduced by the glitter and desiring it and watching my hand move out to grab it, some part of me knew I could never wear it. In looking back on the experience, I recognize that the predominant energy was seeing something attractive and wanting it for myself. Even at that age, there was something distorted in the urge. That seven-year-old did not understand that she was already beautiful. For many of us, the desire for things outside of ourselves, unless held in Right Understanding, becomes harmful or causes us to break ethical guidelines. It is not that we are bad people but just that we misunderstand that we are beautiful already. Our spiritual practice teaches us what obscures this reality and what uncovers it. — AW

As we come more and more into touch with a sense of ourselves as beautiful, we feel less compulsion to seek things outside of ourselves through unethical actions. Buddhism understands that we are inherently good and can cultivate a way of living that brings us increasingly into connection with our goodness. Buddhist practitioners do not rely on any external authority or source for salvation. We are already "saved," and we can discover that ourselves through the practices of the Eightfold Path. Ethical action underlies these transformative practices.

Right Speech and Right Action: The Five Precepts

All religions have ethical guidelines for laypeople. In Buddhism these guidelines are known as the *Five Precepts,* and they are the foundation for Right Action and Right Speech. The Five Precepts are:

- Abstain from taking life.
- Abstain from taking what is not given.
- Abstain from false speech.
- Abstain from sexual misconduct.
- Abstain from taking intoxicants.

The precepts describe a mind at rest, with no thoughts of gaining, so that in each moment we see things as they are. Take a moment to imagine inheriting a fortune and having a lot of things—beautiful clothes, swimming pools, houses, cars, boats, and so on. Then think of your life as it really is, without all those things. Can you have the perspective to say, "This is how it is: I have only certain things, and that is just how it is"? Nothing else—no desire, no aversion, no envy, no jealousy. When we can see the world from the perspective that things are just as they are, our minds and hearts are at rest. The precepts are an expression of that peace, and they also are the invitation to practice that can bring it to its fullest expression.

THE FIRST PRECEPT: Abstain from Taking Life

The First Precept establishes a sense of nonharming, in which there is no separation between ourselves and others. We are in a relationship of compassion and kindness for all beings. This precept invites us to respect all life—not just large life but even little life, such as mosquitoes.

My partner and I have empty containers in some of our rooms so that in the summer, when mosquitoes get into the house, we can catch them and take them outside. "Mosquito rescue" is a challenge when I am exhausted and have just collapsed in bed and then one starts buzzing around my head. It feels like an unthinkable discipline to put on the light, try to catch the mosquito, take it downstairs, go outside, open the container, and come back in again. This discipline came about at a retreat where I was meditating in my room. A mosquito kept buzzing around trying to bite me, and swishing it away was disturbing my meditation. In a moment of deep frustration, I grabbed my slipper and smashed the mosquito against the wall, its body bloody and squished. In that instant, I saw my mind—the energy of killing, very contracted and hard and aggressive. I was shocked. I did not want to live with that energy inside of me, and I did not want to support it or grow it. Out of that experience, I formally took the vow not to take any life intentionally. This does not mean that I have not accidentally taken life—I have, but it has never been on purpose. This vow is one of the places where love has really grown in my heart. — AW

Not taking life, like the other precepts, can become an opportunity for us to examine what we use in our life and how we use it. So, for example, our choice of laundry detergents and soaps affects life in our waters. How much paper we use and buying products with excessive packaging affects how many trees are logged.

THE SECOND PRECEPT: Abstain from Taking What Is Not Given

The Second Precept bestows the gift of safety. When we practice it in retreat communities, for example, we do not have to lock doors but know that our belongings are secure. Once on a silent retreat at the Insight Meditation Society, someone found a hundred-dollar bill near the bulletin board and thumbtacked it up on the board. There it stayed for a number of days. Finally, the owner took it down and left a thank-you note in its place.

Although few of us would go into a friend's house and take something that was not given to us, the Second Precept means that we would never take *anything* unless it was freely offered to us. Living by this precept can expand into a broad practice of looking deeply into the interrelationship of all life and investigating how our actions might affect it. If you look closely, you can see the implications every time you go shopping. For example, in one store, you may see cheap, attractive clothes that were made in a foreign sweatshop. You can ask yourself if you want instead to buy clothes that are more expensive but that were made by people who were paid better wages, or perhaps secondhand clothes. It can be a hard decision if you do not have much money. There is no right or wrong answer. Rather, abstaining from taking what is not given is an opportunity to investigate our desires and to see if what we need is different from what we want.

THE THIRD PRECEPT: Abstain from False Speech

We rarely think about the tremendous power of speech, but words can bring about peace or war. They can bring people to suicide or to the transmission of the Dharma. The Third Precept, Right Speech, involves abstaining from lying, from speaking without care, and from gossiping in a way that creates negative energy.

We can become devoted to the truth and worthy of other people's confidence. Imagine never knowingly speaking a lie for our own or another person's advantage. The Buddha's teaching on telling the truth is clearly expressed in a story in which he was talking to his son, Rahula, who at the time was a young novice. Pointing to a bowl containing a tiny amount of water, the Buddha said, "So *little*, Rahula, is the spiritual achievement of one who is not afraid to speak a lie." Then the Buddha threw the water away and said, "In the same way, one who tells a deliberate lie throws away whatever spiritual achievements he's made. Do you see now how this bowl is empty? In the same way, one who has no hesitation about speaking lies is empty of spiritual achievement." Then he turned the bowl upside down and said, "See, Rahula, how this bowl has been turned upside down? In the same way, one who tells an intentional lie turns his spiritual achievements upside down and becomes incapable of progress." Further, the Buddha said that in the course of the training for enlightenment, the *bodhisattva*—one who is committed to reducing the suffering and bringing about the enlightenment of all beings—can break all of the precepts except the pledge to speak the truth. This statement reveals just how significant is the commitment to truth telling. Often when we think of our spiritual practice, we think of sitting on a cushion and meditating. Rarely do we think about our speech and the impact it has on us.

Speaking the truth is at the heart of Insight Meditation practice. As we become more mindful, we start to refrain from moving with greed, hatred, and delusion, which so obscure what is true. And as we make a commitment to speaking the truth, we open our hearts and minds.

The Buddha also urged us to abstain from speaking negatively, so that we do not cause dissension but rather unite our circle of friends and community, becoming a conciliator of enemies and a creator of friends. The Buddha's vision of Right Speech includes speaking words that create peace, that are pleasant to hear, and that are spoken at the proper time. All these admonitions could be summarized as speaking only what is both true and useful.

Our investigation into Right Speech also includes a consideration of gossiping. Gossiping is often the communication of our judgments, self-righteousness, and opinions. It is how we define ourselves relative to others, separating some people as "good" from others who are "bad." Have you noticed how easy it is, in a conversation, to be critical of people who are not present? Not only does the act of gossiping hurt us, but the damage it causes others can be immense when the gossip gets out into the world, where it seems to have a life of its own, beyond the control of those who started it. The story was told many years ago in a small Russian village of a man who went to his rabbi, filled with remorse for having spread rumors about a neighbor. When the man asked if there were any way he could make up for the harm he had caused, the rabbi gave him very specific instructions: "Go to market in the next village and buy a chicken to bring to me. As you walk back with it, pluck it so that it has no feathers at all when you get it here." The man did as he was told and several hours later returned with a completely denuded chicken. He handed the chicken to the rabbi and asked what he should do next. "You should go back to the market," the rabbi said, "and as you retrace your steps, gather up every one of the feathers." "But that's impossible," the man said. The rabbi merely nodded.

In this precept, the Buddha asked us to look particularly at what our intentions are in relationship to speech. Are we creating suffering for ourselves or others? When do we lie and why? Is it because we want something so badly that truth does not feel important? Do we distort because we are angry and need to justify our position? Are we lying for no particular reason—telling an irrational lie? Or exaggerating for the sake of joking or telling a good story because we want to be seen as entertaining or good humored? If we are gossiping, is it because we do not feel too good about ourselves and want to paint someone in a dark light? Do we engage in gossip because we are feeling bored?

We can extend Right Speech to include listening. Giving attention is one of the purest expressions of love. When we give each other the gift of listening with our whole hearts, separation dissolves and hurt is healed.

Do we remain silent when we could speak out? Many of the people we respect have spoken out for justice—Harriet Tubman, Martin Luther King, Jr., Thich Nhat Hanh, perhaps the minister of a local Unitarian Universalist congregation, or someone who spoke up for us when we were being teased at school. Their gift of courage has changed our lives.

As we discovered in our investigation of karma, it is our intentions that create goodwill and kindness. Suppose a person brandishing a knife is searching for someone in a brown coat. If we say we have not seen the person when in truth we have, we are lying in the service of peace and kindness.

The power of words can also manifest the best of our intentions, as in the beautiful prayer attributed to Francis of Assisi:

> Make me an instrument of your peace. Where there is hatred, let me sow love. Where there is injury, pardon. Where there is discord, unity. Where there is doubt, faith. Where there is error, truth. Where there is despair, hope. Where there is sadness, joy. Where there is dark-ness, light. Grant me that I may not so much seek to be consoled as to console, to be understood as to understand, to be loved as to love. For it is in giving that we receive. It is in pardoning that we are pardoned. It is in dying that we are born into eternal life [or freedom].

May the power of our words support all that is most loving and wise in ourselves and others.

THE FOURTH PRECEPT: Abstain from Sexual Misconduct
The Fourth Precept asks us to abstain from sexuality that brings harm and from using any power we might have to force

sex against someone's wishes. It encourages us to look at the nature of desire to see when it is part of intimacy—the affirmation of our own and others' humanity—and when it distances us from ourselves and others. Sexuality without intimacy may bring pleasurable physical sensations but it also evokes alienation, which creates the conditions for addiction to or an insatiable desire for sexual objects.

Sometimes desire for fullness of heart is distorted into desire for sexual gratification, especially sexual gratification that recognizes no boundaries. Such desire can become twisted into incest, into rape, and into addictive behaviors that bring about shame, guilt, and lies, causing tremendous suffering.

We often think of sex as though it concerns only sexual acts. But sex is about *relationships*, and relationships are about the commitment to living with each other in ways that are kind, in which we hear each other, in which we refrain from hurting through anger or violence, and in which we create a safe environment for each other. Building honest relationships is a never-ending spiritual practice in which sexuality can be a source of deep connection.

THE FIFTH PRECEPT: Abstain from Taking Intoxicants
This precept asks us to refrain from taking intoxicants or mind-altering substances when they bring the mind out of balance. When we drink too much alcohol, the sense of knowing what is right and wrong falls away, and we lose the ability to refrain from harm. If we are angry, that particular quality of consciousness that says, "I'd better go for a walk to work off the anger," is not there. We become identified with and act out that anger. Many beatings, especially in cases of domestic violence, and many car accidents happen when there is intoxication. The fifth precept does not say that we can never

have a glass of wine with dinner. Rather, it invites us to be aware of what happens to our mind when we use too much alcohol or drugs and to avoid allowing this to happen.

The Five Precepts are founded on inquiry, on bringing to each moment the quality of investigation into how to best manifest our intentions of nonharming. This process is well illustrated in an old Zen story in which all the monks in a Japanese monastery repeatedly complained to the abbot that one monk had been stealing. Some months later the stealing was still going on, and the monks came to the abbot outraged. They told the abbot that if he did not make the thief leave, they, the rest of the monastic community, would depart. The abbot said to them, "It is fine if you leave. You understand the difference between what will bring you freedom and what will not, and this monk who is stealing does not, so he needs to remain to learn this." The monks were so moved by the wisdom of the abbot that they remained.

In this story, the abbot was able to extend both compassion and wisdom to teach nonharming. We have the same capacity in relationship to ourselves. If we break a precept, we may feel we have failed and experience self-judgment and shame. We can take responsibility for actions that are harmful, but we never deserve judgment, shame, and guilt. We understand that we have something to learn and can love ourselves at the same time.

Right Livelihood

According to the Buddha, it is helpful to support ourselves and gain wealth in accordance with certain standards. Our source of livelihood best serves us if it is legal rather than illegal, peaceful rather than coercive or violent, and honest rather than deceitful, and if it uses means that do not entail harm or suffering. The Buddha put specific occupations outside of these guidelines: dealing in weapons, dealing in living beings (raising animals for slaughter and butchery, slave trade, and prostitution), dealing in poisons, trafficking in intoxicants, and practicing an occupation that requires cheating.

Right Livelihood includes many aspects of our work life—how we talk to people, how we relate to our work, how we relate to our employers or employees, and how we work with the Five Precepts within the context of our work.

The kinds of challenges we face in making decisions about Right Livelihood are well illustrated in a very old Jewish story. Gabriel was wandering lost in the desert when he spotted a man leading a herd of camels. Half-crazed from thirst, Gabriel crawled up to the man and begged for water. The camel owner refused and left Gabriel to die. Gabriel miraculously managed to get back to a town and in a short time became very wealthy. One day Gabriel learned that a camel dealer was interested in obtaining a loan from him to enlarge his stock. When the man entered his office, Gabriel immediately recognized him as the man who had refused to help him when he was so desperate in the desert.

What would you do if you were Gabriel? Suppose you were in banking and the man seeking the loan was a neighbor who had ignored you when your car had broken down in the middle of the night on a deserted road and you had tried to flag him down. Would you tell him to get out immediately, with the energy of retribution, anger, and blame? Would you feel good saying, "Get out, I'm not going to hear your request—you do not deserve a thing"? Would you grit your teeth, bite your tongue, and go ahead and give this man the loan? What would most bring about peace in yourself and in your community?

Finally, Right Livelihood inquires whether our jobs are nurturing virtue—not just by avoiding producing or selling weapons or intoxicants, but more generally. Does your job support conditions in which skillful qualities can arise?

Exercise: The Precepts

Work with one precept for each of the next five weeks.

1. For each precept, reflect on the events of the day and what you noticed in relation to that precept.

   Notice when you are relating from kindness and when from not caring.

   See if you can refrain from judging yourself during this exploration.

2. Take one aspect of Right Speech and practice it for a week, then continue with the others.

   How does each one feel?

   Can you work with these areas with patience and perseverance?

8. The Eightfold Path: Concentration

During a retreat at her desert center, Ruth Denison took us outside to do seeing meditation with the magnificent sunset. I was standing there watching the shades of red streaking through the sky, open to the experience of red, and Ruth said, "Drop even the concept of sunset and see what you see." I got it. I understood that what I was seeing was just form and color—it was not even "sunset." But then she said, "Notice the telephone pole." I suddenly realized that just a few feet away was an ugly telephone pole. It had been coated with tar to preserve the wood, and it had a bad smell. It was right in front of me, but I had not seen or smelled it. I realized I had not seen it because I considered it ugly and had just pushed it out of my experience. I began to ask myself, "How much else have I missed because it has been unpleasant?" It came to me in that moment how judgmental I had been of Germans during World War II because I could not *believe they had not seen the concentration camps. I finally understood how that process of not seeing can be unconscious because something is unpleasant. — AW*

Cultivating the ability to see both the sunset and the telephone pole involves not only the presence of pleasant or unpleasant feelings but also a balance of effort, mindfulness, and concentration, which we will investigate in this chapter.

....

Right Effort

Right Effort is the energy we need for our practice—the energy to be mindful and to refrain from hurting ourselves or others. It is the effort to find a book about Insight Meditation and read it. Without Right Effort, it does not matter how much knowledge we have collected about the teachings of the Buddha; we will not be able to develop the skillful qualities of mind and heart that can bring about our transformation. Instead, we will just keep repeating our habitual patterns endlessly. The Buddha described four ways we can make courageous effort: guarding, abandoning, nurturing, and maintaining.

GUARDING

Guarding means becoming sensitive to conditions that evoke unskillful energies. Many such situations occur in our everyday lives: rushing to get somewhere on time, commuting in heavy traffic, going to bed late and becoming overtired, skipping meals, drinking too much alcohol, not taking enough time to rest, or repressing feelings. Guarding our minds means making an effort to avoid these conditions and, when we cannot, paying close attention so that unskillful energies do not arise.

ABANDONING

We can abandon unskillful energies once they have arisen, but it takes courage to drop the familiar and to open ourselves to the unknown. The hindrances are especially seductive in making us believe that if we just go along with unskillful energies or increase them, we will experience some kind of release. It takes tremendous effort to unhook ourselves from our habitual story lines and patterns of anger, desire, fear, anxiety, envy, and jealousy. We have to call forth parts of ourselves that might feel hidden and say to ourselves, "I don't know if I can, but I summon the best of myself to let go of these negative energies." In the very next instant, we may again be right in the middle of our "he said this," "she did this," story line. And again we must call on courageous effort to let go. Our motivation for abandoning our story lines is our knowledge that they cannot bring us happiness. As our practice deepens, we see more and more clearly that they can bring us only one thing: suffering.

What hooks us into negative story lines and feeds these unskillful states? *Blame.* Blaming someone or some situation nourishes our unskillful mental energies. It locks us into a victim position because we hold someone or some experience responsible for our feelings. In fact, no one can make us feel or think anything. Only we are responsible for the feelings and thoughts that arise. When we blame, we give up our capacity to choose—we give up our freedom. But no matter how difficult an experience is, we have the ability to relate to it with equanimity. This ability has been exemplified for decades by the Dalai Lama, who has blamed the Chinese not once for the persecution of Tibetans but instead has worked diligently for peace.

How do we abandon blame? The first step is to drop the story line and open to our feelings. Blame is often an aversion to experiencing our own feelings, which we have projected onto something else. If you have trouble acknowledging these feelings with kindness, it might be helpful to connect with your *intention to acknowledge* them by saying phrases such as "May I hold this anger [fear, anxiety, etc.] with kindness. May this feeling be embraced by my heart." If you are able to open your heart and hold with kindness your experience, whatever it is, the difficult emotions will lose their intensity. Once you can move in balance, you are able to see the situation more clearly and act if necessary more effectively.

Understanding karma can inspire us to actively abandon unskillful qualities of mind. When we experience negative energies, we can feel how unpleasant they are, and we know that acting them out waters the "seeds in our storehouse," creating more such energies in the future.

The Buddha included three other techniques for abandoning unskillful energies. First, we can think of the positive qualities associated with the person or experience that triggered our negative reaction. If this does not work, we can just pay no attention to these thoughts and energies because they are impermanent and will change. Finally, we can "suppress them, root them out, or clench our teeth and press our tongue against our gums."

Many times when I was young, I clenched my teeth to avoid saying something horrible. During the 1970s and 1980s, with the popular growth of psychology and psychotherapy, people thought that repressing all our negative emotions was not only unhealthy but actually bad for our mental health. For myself, I found that my old mechanisms of repression came out of self-judgment and hatred—beliefs such as "It is bad to feel this anger" or "I am a bad person for feeling this anger." I do think it is unhealthy to repress our feelings out of negativity or shame. But that is not what abandoning the unskillful *means. Today, pressing my tongue against the roof of my mouth to avoid saying something unskillful comes out of self-love and respect. I do not want to hurt myself by solidifying or supporting the growth of unskillful energies. I also do not want to hurt others. The effort that springs from self-love becomes a great protection and gift for us all.* — AW

NURTURING AND MAINTAINING
Nurturing is the third way to make courageous effort; it refers to arousing positive mental qualities, particularly the seven factors of enlightenment: mindfulness, investigation, effort, rapture, tranquillity, concentration, and equanimity (see pages 130–132). The fourth way is to maintain, increase, and develop the skillful qualities that have already arisen.

There are several traditional ways of arousing effort. One is to reflect on the states of misery that appear when we do not cultivate effort. Another is to reflect on the benefits of arousing effort. When our situation seems impossible, we can recall all those who are walking this path with us, those who are practicing in prisons and hospitals, and those who practice the Dharma in countries where it is illegal. If they can do it, so can we.

We can also contemplate the blessings of being able to make an effort to build virtue. Simply by having the desire to manifest the vision in our hearts, we are blessed. Many beings are so far from having that desire, they think that stealing or murdering is going to make them happy.

We can also arouse effort by thinking of our teachers and of what the Buddha achieved. We can remember the faith that our teachers and our friends have in us. We can avoid those friends who do not support our efforts. Reflecting on the beauty of our faith, our morality, our knowledge of the Dharma, our generosity, and our wisdom also generates effort.

There are times to make effort and times to back off, relax, and let go. When you are caught in a powerful depression, anxiety, or rage, or when you are feeling as though there is not much point to anything, this is the time to make the immense effort required to work with very difficult mind states. Some of the ways to do this were enumerated in chapter 3. What is most important on this path of transformation is to remember that you *can* do it and that making the effort is the first and most important step.

I have found many ways to work with difficult mind states. The worst time for me is often in the middle of the night when I cannot go to sleep. If I notice frustration because I can't sleep, I make myself get up and do walking meditation. It is the last thing I want to do. It is cold outside my bed, I feel tired, and I do not want to get up, but I also know that unless I make an effort, things will just get worse. So I bundle up and go into the kitchen and start walking. I have also found walking outside very helpful. Once I am walking, I still have to make tremendous effort to keep bringing my mind back to the sensations of walking, but it is not quite as hard as getting out of bed. I dedicate each step and the effort to be present to those who cannot walk—those in wheelchairs, those in small cells, and those who are too sick.

I keep rededicating every time I lose energy. It has also been help-ful to share the merit of my practice—sharing all the benefits and purity of my efforts with others, so each moment of practice becomes a gift to the universe. — AW

Most of us already know some of the things that help us "come back into connection" with ourselves. When we hold a vision of what is possible for us through this process, we can act on our intention to practice and trust the practice to take care of us.

In contrast to making too little effort, sometimes we try too hard and we become tense. When this happens, we have become goal-oriented in our practice and are straining to "get somewhere." One symptom of too much effort is searching for and straining to examine our experience rather than settling back and letting our experience touch us. This is the time to back off, and remember the Buddha's emphasis on the Middle Way. "Right" Effort means wise or appropriate effort. Finding the right level of effort takes time—and the "right level" changes in different situations. Over time you will become attuned to what you need. You must be patient with yourself as you go through the process of discovery.

If you are working with trauma or painful experiences from childhood, you must be especially sensitive to the quality of your effort. In such situations, where the usual boundaries and defenses are often not in place, the mind can be extremely impressionable. If you find yourself working with states of dis-sociation or disintegration in connection with these areas, please go very slowly and take many breaks.

The whole Dharma community and the wider sangha appreciate all the efforts you make. Each effort is a precious gift to yourself and to all of us. Reading this chapter and book requires an effort. Perhaps you would like to take this opportunity right now to appreciate your efforts.

Right Mindfulness

If you were driving on a moonless night without headlights, it would be impossible to see where you were going. You would have to put on headlights. Mindfulness is like turning the headlights on our world on a dark night. It illuminates our experience, brings it into focus, and keeps it there. Mindfulness sees what is happening without distortions. It dispels confusion and fog. If we cannot see where we are going, how do we know it is the right path? How do we know we are not speeding down the road toward a crash and suffering?

As we saw in chapter 2, the Buddha described two kinds of mindfulness: *bare attention*, that quality of knowing directly and intimately the essentials of an experience without interpretation; and *general comprehension*, which understands the purpose of what we are doing. When we meditate, we use bare attention to know our breath, while general comprehension is our understanding of why we are meditating. Bare attention is the predominant aspect of mindfulness when we meditate— knowing the coolness and tingling as the air passes into our nostrils. General comprehension is the predominant aspect of mindfulness in our daily lives—when we go out the front door in the morning, we know where we are going and why.

THE FOUR FOUNDATIONS OF MINDFULNESS

In his teachings, the Buddha divided our experiences into four areas—body, feelings (sensations of pleasantness and unpleasantness and neither pleasantness nor unpleasantness), mind factors (emotions), and mind objects (the core teachings of the Buddha)—called the *Four Foundations of Mindfulness* (see pages 196–206 for the text). Practicing mindfulness in each of these foundations is sufficient to bring about freedom and awakening.

The First Foundation: Body

The body is a wonderful place to turn to in the practice of mindfulness. With the body, a variety of different practices are possible—mindfulness of the breath, of sensation in the whole body, of movement in stretching and bending, of bodily functions such as eating and urinating, and of death. A special benefit of this First Foundation to mindfulness is that bodily experiences are accessible. Our bodies are always with us, expressing our life-force in our breath, temperature, pressure, vibrations, and so on. Our direct connection to these experiences frees us of our stories and preferences, and becomes a good training ground for mindfulness.

The Buddha began this teaching with mindfulness of breathing, which is not only the starting point for most Buddhist meditation practice but also the common training for Insight Meditation. He gave simple instructions, inviting us to put aside "worldly grief and greed"—that is, all the worries, lists, and unsettled matters in our daily life—and to mindfully breathe in and mindfully breathe out. In the formal meditation practice of mindfulness to our breath, we know whether our breath is short or long, hard or soft.

Our breath is an ideal refuge. It is our immediate source of life—without it we would die in a very few minutes. It is part of our ongoing exchange with the universe, and we join much of life in this exchange. Wherever we are, whatever we are doing—in an office, on a construction site, waiting tables—we are always breathing, and we can mindfully connect with our breath over and over again.

Our bodies provide us with myriad other invitations to practice mindfulness. Wherever we are and whatever we are doing, we can be mindful of our bodies. If, for example, you reach for a sweater on the top shelf of your closet, you can feel the stretch along your side. You can sense your weight shifting to the balls of your feet as you go onto your tiptoes. You can connect with the fact that you are seeing your sweaters, how they are folded, their form, and their colors. You might connect with the smell of slight mustiness because you do not often wear a particular sweater, or the faint aroma of laundry detergent if you do.

Whatever you are doing—stretching, bending, sitting, standing—you can use your posture as a way to come back into connection with yourself. Whatever you are seeing, hearing, smelling, or touching, your senses provide you with wonderful opportunities to come into the present moment. You can also use other bodily functions, such as urinating and defecating, as occasions for mindfulness.

When we bring mindfulness to the First Foundation, we can experience in our daily lives the four qualities of the universe: earth, air, fire, and water. The Buddha described how these qualities express themselves as softness/pressure (earth), hot/cold (fire), connectedness (water), and vibration (air). We sense pressure, for example, when we are holding a cup, stepping on the earth, or feeling the water in the shower; we sense temperature in the cycle of the seasons and even in the internal sense of heat that results from eating or not eating. In this way, we begin to sense the interplay of the elements and their expression as life.

The Buddha taught a number of other practices related to

mindfulness of the body. One especially powerful technique is to contemplate death. In this contemplation, you think through the stages of dying: You think about being sick and starting to feel your energy dwindling; imagine a lack of consciousness; envision your body disintegrating; contemplate being either burned or put into the earth; and see the end result of ashes or dust.

It is one thing to read about the Buddha sending his monks to the charnel grounds to contemplate death and quite another to be lying in a hospital bed thinking it is happening to me. I was so weak that I was fairly immobilized, and I kept falling asleep, or perhaps losing consciousness. Twice my vision failed, the world around me grew dark, and I thought, "So this is what it's like." My mind was fairly clear, and I kept thinking about a line I had heard Jack Kornfield say: "At your last moment, with your last breath, you probably will not think, 'I should have gone to the office earlier.' " Even a workaholic like me did not think about the office. I felt kind of sad—there were still so many things I had meant to do—but I was not afraid. Most of all, I just felt interested in the changes I was experiencing, in a detached way, and was rather shocked that it really was happening to me. As it turned out, this was not my time to die, but the effect of coming so close was to radically change the way I related to myself and to other people. I really got impermanence, I think for the first time. — JS

The Buddha asked us to contemplate death because he recognized how attached we are to our bodies, how we think that this body is *our* body. As we become aware of the different sensations of the breath coming and going, we can experience the impermanence of breath without claiming it as "our" breath. In the same way, while we are aware of breath, we can connect in that moment with the whole body's coming into being and dying in a universal process independent of any "I."

The Buddha's teaching about the body's impermanence is dramatically illustrated in the story of Sundari-Nanda, a kinswoman who became one of the Buddha's main followers during his lifetime. This Indian noblewoman, renowned for her beauty, dressed in elegant silk saris and spent her time combing her hair and pampering her body. When she first went to see him, the Buddha—who was said to have many psychic powers—saw into her mind and found faith, generosity, lovingkindness, and other skillful qualities in addition to attachment to her own physical beauty. Sundari-Nanda saw seated next to the Buddha an exact replica of herself, which he had caused to materialize. As she stared, the likeness began to age. Her face got old and wrinkled, her hair became gray and frizzy, one side of her mouth drooped, she started to drool, she became bent over, and her breasts sagged. In seeing herself grow old in that way and understanding that she actually had nothing to hold on to, she was liberated.

Jack Kornfield tells another story that illustrates the liberation that comes when we let go of our attachment to the idea of "our" permanent body. A young man lost his leg at the hip because of bone cancer. At first he went through tremendous grief and rage. His doctor had him draw pictures of his feelings, and he drew a vase, which represented his body. In the middle of the vase was a deep black crack. Several years later, the man visited his doctor, who took out the vase picture and said, "This one is not finished. Why don't you finish it?" The young man picked up a yellow crayon, put his finger where the crack was, and said, "You see where it is broken? That is where the light comes through." With the yellow crayon he then drew light streaming through the crack into the vase.

This image is a potent reminder that we can find a deep sense of well-being and inner connection even when we are physically challenged. Perhaps you have lost your sight, your hearing, or your mobility, or you are suffering from a severe chronic or acute illness. When you are faced with such difficulties, you are forced to let go of some physical ability. With that letting go, the light begins to stream through, the light of inner connection and well-being.

When we allow our bodies to live without the constraints of ownership, we can love and respect them without judgment, free of the cultural conditioning of what is considered attractive. Just as we appreciate all forms of water—little creeks, rushing rivers, and large bodies of water—so we can come to a natural appreciation of the diversity of our bodily expressions. Each one is deserving of honor.

The Second Foundation: Feelings

In every waking moment, we have contact between one of our sense bases—eyes, ears, nose, tongue, skin, or mind—and an object. We experience all of these contacts as pleasant, unpleasant, or neither pleasant nor unpleasant. With pleasantness comes liking. With unpleasantness comes not liking. With neither pleasantness nor unpleasantness comes fogginess or boredom. With liking (unless there is also mindfulness) comes grasping. With not liking comes aversion. With neither pleasantness nor unpleasantness comes delusion. Think about what happens when you are meditating and experiencing your breath. In every moment the mind is moving either toward or away from the experience. Either you are thinking, "I do not like this. I do not know what I'm doing here. This is just driving me nuts. I can't wait to get out of here." Or "Why doesn't the teacher shut up? This is such a pleasant sensation—I don't want to be distracted."

Whether a particular moment is pleasant, unpleasant, or neither pleasant nor unpleasant is usually karmically set. The feeling is most often determined by our past, and it is different for different people. Some people love to walk by a stormy ocean, but other people are afraid and find a raging coast unpleasant. Some people like warm climates and move down to Florida. Others do not like the heat and live farther north.

Feelings are a critical part of our experience because if we are unconscious of these sensations, they can develop into craving or aversion—the mental factors that bring suffering into our lives. We may be shocked to discover how much time we spend trying to manipulate unpleasant and pleasant sensations. It is not just that we try to control these elements, but the stories that arise out of these experiences can absorb our energy and our attention. For example, suppose that while Jerry is meditating, he has a pain in his knee and it is unpleasant. Because of the experience of unpleasantness, the mind is off and running: "Maybe something serious is happening to my knee. Maybe I should go into the hospital. Maybe I've inherited the arthritis that Dad and Granddad had. I should probably stop doing meditation right away and think about going to an osteopath and supplementing my diet with those new antioxidants." We can go on and on, creating stories about our lives and what we should be doing—all based on one sensation. It is remarkably freeing to catch ourselves when we are embroiled in our stories and to tell ourselves, "This is just unpleasant. That's all it is."

The third category, neither pleasant nor unpleasant sensation, is sometimes described as neutral. When this feeling comes up we often find ourselves either drifting off into other "more interesting" thoughts or becoming bored. Like the other feelings it is difficult to stay present with the experience.

At the same time, we do not have to repress the natural joy that arises through our senses. In her poem "The Sun," Mary Oliver asks if we have seen anything more wonderful than the evening sun floating toward the horizon, or the morning sun "like a red flower / streaming upward on its heavenly oils." She asks if we have ever felt anything like the love we feel in the universe every day. When we become more present and more open to eating an orange or watching a beautiful sunset, we feel not only a deeper pleasure in the experience but also less attachment and disappointment when it ends.

The Third Foundation: Mind Factors

The Third Foundation is what we call the world of emotions and what the Buddha called the fifty-two mental factors or qualities of the mind. The skillful mental factors include faith, mindfulness, fear of wrong, generosity, lovingkindness, equanimity, tranquillity, lightness of body and consciousness, Right Speech, Right Action, Right Livelihood, compassion, sympathetic joy, and wisdom. As we will see in chapter 9, cultivating these qualities is a deliberate practice that enables us to let go of envy, avarice, delusion, and hatred. Among the fourteen unskillful energies are three that are almost always present when we experience suffering: delusion, or mental blindness to what brings us suffering and causes unwise attention; fearlessness, or not understanding the consequences of harmful actions, speech, or thoughts; and restlessness, especially compulsive planning. Other factors that bring us suffering include greed, conceit, hatred, envy, avarice, worry, sloth and torpor, and doubt—some of which we have already met in the discussion of challenges to meditation and life (chapter 3).

The fact that we are practicing on a spiritual path does not mean that we should try to repress unskillful factors when they arise. For example, if you are feeling agitated, you can recognize the agitation as agitation, to know the experience of agitation, and to relate to it as a friend: "Oh, agitation. I see you again." Being mindful sometimes takes courage and commitment because it is often easier to repress unskillful factors than to feel them. But the purification of our hearts and minds will come about only through opening up to the experience of whatever is arising. It is critical in this process not to get involved in the story line around the mental factors that arise.

After the painful breakup of a long-term relationship, I felt like one big roiling ball of unskillful mind factors. They seemed to come up worst for me at night. So I kept my meditation cushion on the bed. When they clobbered me, I would roll over and sit on my cushion. I said to myself, "No plots. Just the feeling. Oh, it is grief. What does grief feel like? It is really hot. It is burning at the bottom of my throat. I feel like there is a sumo wrestler sitting on my chest." After a few minutes of intimately knowing my grief, I would find that it had lessened, and I could bring my awareness to my breathing. — JS

After a while we begin to see that grief is not just *our* grief but a universal phenomenon like the wind, which sometimes moves into hurricane force, or softens like breath. Seeing grief as something experienced universally can help us bring ourselves into a more balanced relationship to it. As we see such mental factors arising and passing away, we begin to see their impermanence. That feeling of being hooked into them starts to disintegrate, and we are freer of the storminess of their energies.

The Fourth Foundation: Mind Objects

In the Fourth Foundation of Mindfulness, the Buddha invited us to examine the core teachings of the Dharma:

- The five hindrances: desire, ill will, sloth and torpor, restlessness, and doubt (pages 33–50)
- The five aggregates: form, feeling, perception, mental formations, and consciousness (pages 69–71)
- The *six sense organs*, or *bases:* eyes, ears, nose, tongue, body, and mind
- The *seven factors of enlightenment:* mindfulness, investigation, effort, rapture, tranquillity, concentration, and equanimity (pages 130–132)
- The Four Noble Truths: suffering, the origin of suffering, the cessation, and the way leading to it (chapter 5)

The Buddha encouraged us to investigate our experience using these core teachings. For example, suppose you are washing dishes late at night and find yourself becoming irritable and having thoughts such as "How come I'm always doing the dishes? It's not fair." The more you think about it, the more irritable you become, and the more ill will you feel. The Fourth Foundation of Mindfulness shows how you can investigate the contents of your mind with bare attention and see ill will as an unskillful mental quality, one of the hindrances. You can go further and ask yourself what conditions give rise to this ill will. You can see that you are very tired and needed to be in bed hours ago. When you bring this general understanding to your situation, the ill will eases until it disappears, and you can then cultivate equanimity. You are aware that the qualities of bare attention, investigation, and equanimity are now present in your mind—but you also know that if they disappear in the next moment because you are back into your irritable thoughts, you can notice that too.

Another way to work with the Fourth Foundation is to select one of the five aggregates—form, feeling, perception, mental formations, and consciousness—and to contemplate it as your meditation practice.

THE SEVEN FACTORS OF ENLIGHTENMENT

In English the term *enlightenment* has many meanings, but the Buddha used it specifically to refer to Nirvana (page 78). We can cultivate the conditions in which enlightenment can arise, known as the *seven factors of enlightenment:* mindfulness, investigation, effort, rapture, tranquillity, concentration, and equanimity. Investigation, effort, and rapture are called the arousing factors; tranquillity, concentration, and equanimity are called the stabilizing or calming factors. Mindfulness is the conductor of the group. The Buddha said that the practice of mindfulness can bring about the six other factors, but we can also practice cultivating these factors independently.

As we become increasingly aware of our mind states, we can begin to discern which factors are arising and where there might be an imbalance. When the mind is tired, for example, we can cultivate energy or effort. When the mind is excited, we know we need to calm down. The factors of enlightenment are an expression of a mind in balance.

o *Mindfulness* creates the conditions to keep the other factors in balance. When mindfulness becomes strong, it calls forth investigation.

o *Investigation* helps us to go beyond the surface of things to discover the underlying laws of the universe and the three characteristics that the Buddha described as *dukkha*, *anicca*, and *anatta*, the Pali words for "unsatisfactoriness," "impermanence," and "selflessness." Investigation helps us to see the unsatisfactoriness described in the First Noble Truth and the expression of selflessness, the freedom from clinging, described in the Third Noble Truth. As we practice the Eightfold Path, investigation helps us to see our experience in such detail that we come to recognize the law of impermanence. Investigation can counter boredom and aversion by lighting up the mind with questions such as "What is my experience?" "What are the details of it?" "Do I really know it?" Investigation creates the conditions for effort to arise.

o *Effort* gives us the energy to practice. The fire of effort gives the energy for rapture to arise.

o *Rapture* is joyous interest that pervades the mind and body with lightness and happiness, making the mind malleable. Because there is rapture, there is mental comfort, so we want to continue our practice. Rapture brings about the conditions for tranquillity.

o *Tranquillity* can cool a mind filled with agitation and bring the refreshment of peace. When strong, it can suppress remorse and anxiety. It follows rapture but can also be cultivated by creating a comfortable climate in which to practice. Tranquillity provides the conditions for concentration to grow.

o *Concentration* (which we will speak of in the next section) is the mind gathered and directed in a continuous way toward an object. Concentration brings the space for equanimity to arise.

o *Equanimity* is balance; it is a mind without clinging or aversion, so it is not inclined toward any extreme but remains centered (see pages 151–154).

Thus, our beginning attempts to practice mindfulness also begin to create the circumstances for the seven factors of enlightenment. The Buddha asked us therefore to make awareness of these factors part of our practice, to cultivate, regulate, and balance them not only in our meditation practice but also throughout our lives.

....

Right Concentration

In order to develop concentration, we are asked to renounce whatever takes us away from it. In chapter 7, we saw that Right Speech, Right Action, and Right Livelihood provide the guidelines and supportive conditions for developing Right Concentration. We can develop concentration through our mindfulness practice and, according to the Buddha's discourses, also through creating order and keeping our environment and bodies clean.

When we first learn to meditate, our minds often jump around all over the place. One of the factors that brings stability and calm is concentration, or one-pointedness of mind. In each moment that we are conscious of something—a taste, smell, thought, sight—concentration unifies and directs the mind toward knowing it. Concentration brings an unbroken attentiveness to our experience and counteracts the tendency of the mind to perceive in fragments distorted by ripples of random thoughts. Imagine watching a sheepdog herding lambs, making sure they all go in one direction, rounding up those who begin to stray. Our minds are usually like a herd of sheep with no dog, wandering here and there in one direction after another. We need enormous effort to gather our stray thoughts and impulses, but when we do, we experience the benefits of concentration.

Concentration calms the mind when we are agitated and brings stability for insight. The walking and breath-counting meditations using numbers and counting up to ten (described in chapters 2 and 3, respectively) are especially effective concentration techniques to calm the mind. Another calming concentration practice uses the divine abodes, which are described in chapter 9.

You have tasted the power of concentration when you were so focused on something that you let go of other activities and became absorbed in the experience at hand. If you were engrossed in watching a ball game or painting a picture, you did not hear the phone ring or perhaps feel any discomfort in your body. One of the blessings of concentration is that it temporarily neutralizes the five hindrances. In this way it creates the conditions for absorption to grow stronger and for rapture and happiness to arise.

In meditation when we practice focused and continuous attention, we activate five mental factors that counteract the five hindrances. When we *point and focus our minds* toward the breath, for example, the effort counteracts dullness and drowsiness. *Anchoring the mind* on an object drives away doubt. *Rapture* shuts out ill will. *Happiness* excludes restlessness and worry. *One-pointedness* counters sensual desire. The hindrances thus fade away from the mind, although they are not eradicated. Only insight can eliminate them.

Some very quiet states may seem like the calmness that results from concentration but are actually blurred, dreamy, hazy, or ill-defined. When we investigate such states, we find blankness or nonperception. They are not Right Concentration because they lack mindfulness.

Right Effort, Right Mindfulness, and Right Concentration work in tandem, supporting each other and providing the conditions for each to grow. We need effort to cultivate mindfulness and to provide the most supportive conditions for concentration to grow. For its part, mindfulness can detect clearly when we do not have enough mental energy or focus and can direct the mind toward their cultivation. It is like three friends walking down a path together, arms interlinked, supporting each other and giving each other strength over difficult and new terrain. These energies become some of our greatest allies in our quest for freedom.

Exercise: Right Effort

Begin to notice the patterns of when you make an effort in your life and when you do not.

What are the results?

Practice one particular of the four efforts—guarding, abandoning, nourishing, and maintaining—each week for four weeks.

Exercise: The Four Foundations of Mindfulness

Take two weeks to practice each foundation of mindfulness.

Start with the First Foundation, the body. Focus on some specific practices such as bending and stretching, eating, or bathing. Each night write down when you remembered that foundation and how it felt to you.

Notice how you relate to the experience of pleasantness, unpleasantness, or neither. Just keep noticing for a while. Notice how you build on the experience with thoughts and other feelings. Investigate if this process contributes to your happiness.

When you come to the Third Foundation of Mindfulness, notice if any patterns of emotions arise frequently. Take some time to write down what you notice. What happens if you allow the feelings to occur without identifying with or attaching yourself to them?

Begin to contemplate the teachings of the Buddha that you have read about in this book. Do they make sense to you? Take each section in the Fourth Foundation of Mindfulness, and think about it for a few minutes before you meditate. As an alternative, contemplate the subject of each chapter in this book.

For increasing concentration, when you notice your mind wandering while you are in the middle of an activity, try making an effort to come back to what is happening and to remain focused on the activity as long as you are doing it.

See if you can make a determination to remember more each day.

9. Living Practice and the Divine Abodes

On a freezing-cold day in February 1998, I found myself sweating profusely, trembling, and skittering over the icy pavement on legs that could barely hold me up. A few hours later I was in a hospital emergency room, surrounded by doctors and medical students eager to look at a kind of lesion they had seen only in pictures in textbooks. Diagnosis was uncertain, but the doctors were sure that it was one of two rare life-threatening illnesses. At first I felt gratitude that I had returned just the day before from a lovingkindness meditation retreat—that my heart was open and I was experiencing at least a little of the equanimity I needed. Then I realized that what I had to do was simply continue the practices of that retreat. I believe now that if I had left lovingkindness practice behind the walls of the retreat center, I would have never gotten through the hours, days, months, and now years that this illness has battered me. But I have integrated into my practice everything that has arisen for me—from anger at *my body for "letting me down," to fear of pain, to illness from medications, to gratitude for the hundreds of kindnesses with which I've been blessed.* — J S

One of the greatest challenges we face is resisting thoughts that are self-judgmental or tainted with negativity and at the same time opening to our capacity to offer lovingkindness to ourselves and others. The Buddha recognized that it is critical for us to make this heart connection, so he taught four formal practices—so beautiful that they are known as the *divine abodes* (*Brahma-viharas* in Sanskrit and Pali). The divine abodes that we can learn to dwell in are lovingkindness (*metta* in Pali), compassion, sympathetic joy, and equanimity.

A theme throughout this book has been acknowledging the blessings we receive as human beings—perhaps the greatest of which is our capacity to transform ourselves and awaken the qualities of our fundamental nature. Our first step is an ongoing intention to manifest our potential. Through reflection and focusing on certain phrases, we can awaken the innate qualities of lovingkindness, compassion, sympathetic joy, and equanimity, which lie in our heart. Often we feel very disconnected from these energies, and it seems superficial to think about lovingkindness when we feel hatred or to think about the joy of someone's success when we are feeling envy.

Despite such negative feelings, our intention to connect to these positive energies brings about a change in our expression as human beings. This does not just happen in a week or in two months. It occurs slowly over time because over and over again we make the choice to awaken our hearts, to change and put our lives in the service of these positive energies. One of the most beautiful practices for that transformation is lovingkindness meditation practice (see *Metta Sutta*, pages 208–209).

Lovingkindness

The Buddha said of lovingkindness: "Whatever kinds of worldly merit there are, all are not worth one sixteenth part of the heart deliverance of lovingkindness; in shining and beaming and radiance the heart deliverance of lovingkindness far excels them."

As the traditional story goes, the Buddha first taught *metta* to a group of monks who had gone out into a forest to practice. Deep in the woods, they were beset by demons, who terrified them and drove them out of the forest. The alarmed monks ran back to the Buddha and asked to go somewhere else. The Buddha taught them a technique that would protect them from all evil spirits—*metta*—then sent them back into the same forest.

Metta The word *metta*—lovingkindness—welcomes visitors to the Insight Meditation Society, where cofounder Sharon Salzberg has been a strong proponent of *metta* meditation. The word was assembled from letters spelling out the name of the Christian monastery that originally occupied the buildings.

The happy ending to this story is that the monks' lovingkindness totally disarmed the demons, who became their servants. The happy ending for us is that over the centuries, countless meditators have proved that this practice can transform our relationship to ourselves and to others.

In the formal practice of lovingkindness, we work with a few set phrases, directing them to several categories of people in turn: first to ourselves, then to a "benefactor" (often our teacher), a friend, a neutral person, a difficult person, and finally all beings everywhere. How long we practice and which categories of beings we use depend upon our own situation. We might send *metta* to a particular being for a few moments as part of our daily sitting practice or for months or even years within a monastic setting.

The formal phrases of the lovingkindness meditation are:

> May I be free from danger.
> May I have mental happiness.
> May I have physical happiness.
> May I have ease of well-being.

A slightly different variation is:

> May I be safe from inner and outer harm.
> May I be happy and peaceful at heart.
> May I be healthy and strong in body.
> May I take care of myself joyfully in the world.

If these phrases do not work for you, it is fine to use others. Simply find phrases for universal states that you wish for yourself and for others. You might say, for example, "May lovingkindness awaken and suffuse my being, touching and healing all that needs to be healed. May I be free." Or perhaps, "May I be patient. May I be kind to myself. May I embrace all that is difficult. May I love, honor, and respect myself. May I live without fear." At different times, different phrases may work.

When I first started doing metta *practice, I could not send the phrases directly to myself. I had experienced so many traumas as a young child that I felt like I was pushing against a hundred-foot wall. So I decided to send them to a picture of myself as a toddler. I would look at the picture and say, "May you be happy. May you be free from harm and danger. May you live with ease of well-being." I actually spent a month as part of a three-month retreat sending* metta *to that picture of myself.*

I found a way to send lovingkindness to myself as an adult by first accessing my love for nature. I started sending love to the trees and rivers and mountains and birds. After a while the phrases became "May we all be happy. May we all be free from harm." A year later I could come to myself and say, "May I be happy." Sometimes the route is circuitous—it is not linear—and we just have to have patience. I consider myself a hard case, and if I can do it, you can, too. — AW

We can practice lovingkindness formally by spending five, fifteen, thirty, or forty-five minutes, as we do with mindfulness meditation, focusing over and over again on our phrases instead of our breath. When we find that our mind is wandering—or that we are saying the phrases all jumbled up, such as "May I leave with ease" or "May I be filled with fear"—we can have a good laugh, come back again with awareness, and continue.

In the formal practice, after starting with ourselves, we direct these energies toward a person who has helped us in life—a benefactor, perhaps a teacher or a friend. At the beginning of formal training in lovingkindness practice, it is best not to choose a sexual partner or someone toward whom we have complex emotions, including desire, because such feelings can interfere with generating lovingkindness. Instead we choose someone to whom it is very easy to send lovingkindness. We may in fact send it to two people—a benefactor and a friend.

The next category of beings to whom we direct lovingkindness is a neutral person. We often discover at least two things when we reach this stage. First, we do not feel neutral about many people—we tend to have many opinions about people, even if we have never spoken to them. So it is fine to pick a checkout person in a grocery store—especially at a line we do not frequent—a neighborhood gardener, or a shopkeeper. The second thing we may discover is that after we send lovingkindness to a person for even a relatively short time, he or she no longer remains neutral to us. It is astonishing to learn that we can change our feelings about people by sending *metta* to them.

The next kind of person to whom we send *metta* is a difficult person—everyone has at least one in their lives. It may seem very challenging to practice lovingkindness toward someone with whom we are angry or whom we judge. When we are angry with someone, we may think we are seeing them clearly, but we are not. Anger paints people with negativity, so we are actually seeing that person or that situation through distorted lenses.

When I took a new job as head of a corporate division, my biggest challenge was managing a senior employee who was both the most creative and the most difficult person I had ever worked with—for the same reasons. Because of his employment contract, I could fire him, but I could not tell him what to do. Our work styles were so different that I dreaded going to work, and the irritation of his manner made me feel as if I were walking around with a tack coming through my shoe all the time. What I wanted was to create a climate in which he could do the things he did so very well without aggravating the rest of the employees—and me. Every workday morning for five years, I came in, sat down at my desk, thought about his prodigious talent, and did ten minutes of metta *directed to him. Our relationship improved immensely over the years—we became quite fond of each other. He was enormously successful in his work, and he eventually succeeded me as head of the division after I had left the company.* — JS

Contemplating the good qualities of a person with whom we are angry gives us a more realistic perspective of that person. As difficult as it is in the beginning to send lovingkindness to a person we dislike, we can usually think of at least one good quality that he or she has. Perhaps this person said or did a nice thing at one point, or is responsible or punctual. Pondering that one quality is the doorway that opens our heart enough to begin to directly wish this person happiness. We can then begin our formal *metta* practice toward this person. When you are beginning this training, it is helpful to choose a person who is not *too* difficult, then perhaps work up to the most difficult persons in your life later.

One of the greatest obstacles to letting go of aversion toward a difficult person is our fear of letting go of our own needs or integrity. But when we can establish a heart connection with someone we are having difficulty with, we create the ground for communication, and it is in this atmosphere that our needs are most likely to be met.

The final category of beings to whom we send *metta* is all beings everywhere. Once our heart is open from directing *metta* to ourselves and others, we can expand this intention to send the phrases to all beings. Sometimes we may be very specific: "May all women in Afghanistan be happy" or "May all people in Rwanda be happy." We may, as was traditionally done, send *metta* in the six directions (north, south, east, west, above, and below), pausing to contemplate what beings are located in these directions. Bhante Gunaratana of the Bhavana Society sometimes leads *metta* meditations directed to "beings with no legs . . . with two legs . . . with four legs . . . with many legs."

The formal practice of *metta* is a beautiful one to do at any time and in any place. We do not have to sit still or to be in silence, although those conditions are sometimes helpful. Some people who live in New York City have even gotten into the habit of practicing lovingkindness toward other commuters when they are riding the subway to work.

I used to be at my worst driving a car. I was my nastiest, my least generous. When I saw someone waiting to make a turn from a side street, I would not stop but would continue to go on ahead. If there was someone on the sidewalk waiting to cross, my first impulse was to keep on driving through. If someone cut me off or was slow in front of me so that I missed a green light, I started to feel very nasty things about the people in that car. Quite simply, I was a horrible driver. So I took it as my challenge to become less horrible. I tried to practice being kind by saying the following phrases over and over again: "I give thanks for the gift that the Earth has given me in the form of fuel to go to where I need to go. I give thanks to the sky for being an umbrella for me. I hope that all these cars and all the people in front of me are free from danger. May the slow driver in front of me be free from harm. May our use of transportation come into balance. May my little car have a long life." I sent a lot of appreciation to my car for taking me where I needed to go. At the same time I connected to these phrases of kindness, I also reconnected with my body and my understanding that I was sitting and driving. This practice was hugely transforming. — AW

The possibility of coming into a relationship of kindness with all of life—not just human beings—is vast. For example, suppose you recycle plastic bags because you know they endanger the life of some animals. Sometimes it feels like a chore, but you continue to do it as a practice because you know you are giving the gift of kindness to all life by reducing the number of plastic bags. This recycling is part of the practice of lovingkindness.

Ruth Denison taught the lesson of kindness in an unlikely way. She would come into the kitchen when her students were doing dishes—in itself a most unusual act for a teacher—peer over their shoulders, and tell them that they were not being careful enough scrubbing the pots. "What," they asked themselves, "is this meditation teacher doing coming into the kitchen and telling people how to wash pots?" She would give very detailed instructions about which scrubber to use on the inside of the pots and which to use on the copper bottoms. Despite initially being put off, her students soon realized that she was practicing kindness to the pots—that in a way the pots had a life of their own, and she was taking care of them.

Some of us grow up with the attitude that certain things like pots and pans are not important. But the practices of mindfulness and lovingkindness help us to understand that all things deserve care—that when we relate to all things with kindness, we are relating to *ourselves* with kindness. We stop making distinctions such as "I can be kind to you. I do not have to be kind to you. A bed is not that important—I do not have to be kind to a bed." Our caring can become a natural expression of our lives. Lovingkindness as a divine abode is often described as the sun, whose rays shine indiscriminately on the whole Earth and all living things on the Earth. No matter what kind of human being we are—or tree or elephant or violet—the sun's rays find us. The sun does not discriminate between things; nor does lovingkindness put anything outside of its heart. It is an indiscriminate expression of kindness to everything.

One of the obstacles to wide-open loving is attachment, considered the near enemy of lovingkindness. As we have noted, attachment has a tight, grasping quality and creates expectations in our love relationships, such as "I will love you if you do or are such and such," and so we feel justified in not loving our dear ones if they do not live up to our expectations. It is impossible to open our hearts in *metta* and at the same time hold on in attachment. The challenge of intimacy is the challenge of transforming our attachments into *metta*.

The Buddha's invitation to cultivate love is based on his wisdom that when there is judgment, there is aversion, and when there is aversion, it is impossible to see the truth. We may think we are seeing the truth, but judgment, like the hindrances, actually obscures the truth. When we hold ourselves in lovingkindness, it is possible to see clearly and say, "What I did was not very beneficial." There is no self-hatred. There is no sense of shame. There is just a clear assessment of what works and what does not.

At the same time, we can feel remorse for saying or doing something that does not work and that is not healing. But we hold our remorse in kindness. What a gift to give ourselves.

And what a gift to give others when we allow *them* to make mistakes—even big mistakes—and still hold them in our hearts with kindness as well. This ability is tremendously liberating and powerful. For many of us, one of the most profound daily practices can be to whittle away our self-hatred and judgment with lovingkindness so that they arise less and less frequently until they no longer arise at all.

There are said to be eleven benefits of lovingkindness:

One sleeps peacefully.
One wakes peacefully.
One has pleasant dreams.
One is loved by human beings.
One is loved by *devas* (celestial beings) and animals.
One is protected by *devas*.
One is protected from outer harm (fire, poison,
    weapons).
One's mind is joyful and serene.
One has a bright and serene complexion.
One dies peacefully.
One has a fortunate rebirth.

May we each come to reside in our heart's capacity for an infinite friendliness and kindness.

....

Compassion

Compassion is traditionally described as "the quivering of the heart" that arises in response to the pain and suffering that we or other beings are experiencing. It is also a deep befriending of what is difficult inside of ourselves.

Sometimes we do not open our hearts because we feel that if we were to do so, the pain of the world or even what is happening in our own lives would overwhelm us. Part of feeling overwhelmed comes from the idea that we need to lessen or eliminate the pain, that it should not be there at all. We have a sense that suffering is wrong, that we have to do something about it, get rid of it, or even in some way take it on ourselves. But such feelings are not compassion. Compassion understands that pain and difficulty are inherent in the existence of human

Compassion The embodiment of compassion has been depicted as the male *bodhisattva* Avalokiteshvara and as the female Kuan-yin, shown here in a statue at the Insight Meditation Society.

beings and meets with these difficulties in open-hearted sympathy. It is a kind of conjoining, of saying, "I know how this is, and I can stand here with you in unity. I can open my heart and share in the knowing of what it is like to be in pain." We can cultivate compassion by repeating phrases such as "May all beings be free from suffering and pain" and wishing the best for all life.

Pity may look similar to compassion in some ways, but it is distinctly different. In fact, pity is the near enemy of compassion because it contains an element of aversion. Pity is built on the assumption that we ourselves do not experience pain—and so we feel pity for someone else's pain. The Buddha compared the energy of *metta* to that of a mother caring for her only child, but this example also works well for the other divine abodes. As a mother nurtures and takes care of her child, so can we care for all beings. Even though the mother understands the difficulties that will inevitably befall her child, she does not love the child less because of them. Compassion actualizes the same caring. We wish in the most heart-felt way for the reduction of suffering and pain, but at the same time we understand that being alive means that sometimes we experience them.

Co-dependency can also look like compassion: Its expression is giving others caring, and trying to alleviate their suffering. But it is actually very different from compassion because the hidden beliefs underlying co-dependency are that unless we take care of others, we are not lovable, and unless we give unceasingly, we are not worthy. Co-dependency expresses itself as a compulsion to keep giving even when giving takes us out of balance.

The caring of compassion comes from our open-heartedness and sympathy for what is painful and difficult. We do not have a compulsive need to fix the pain of others because we know how to be with pain. We do not lose our balance because we are sustained by our own inner connection, we can distinguish our own needs, and we know when we must meet them.

....

Sympathetic Joy

Sympathetic joy is delight in our own successes and the wish for greater success, as well as pleasure in the success of others. Are these not difficult things to do? Is it not true that many of us, rather than enjoying a success, always play it down? If someone says, "That was great," we say, "It was nothing," or "I didn't try that hard." Having joy for our own successes and having joy for other people's successes is an amazing practice.

Of all of the divine abodes, sympathetic joy may seem the least natural. One of the obstacles to sympathetic joy is the comparing mind, which is its near enemy. When you hear someone talking about their great successes, a little contraction may appear in your heart, and you may hear a voice saying, "How come they are getting it? What about me?" Comparison can produce envy and jealousy, the opposites of sympathetic joy.

When we have no sympathetic joy for ourselves, it is because we are not really honoring ourselves, respecting who we are and how we are. At some level we are sure we are not good enough—and subtle or not, there is the comparison again.

During a retreat at Insight Meditation Society, I heard Joseph Goldstein talk about his struggle with his comparing mind while he was on retreat. He said he was sure everyone was doing much better than he was and was getting special instructions from the teacher that he wasn't getting. During a walking meditation, he saw a bed of flowers alongside the building. Some flowers were in full bloom and others were still budding. As he was seeing them, he understood that, like the flowers, we all have our different times for opening. One is not better than another. — AW

Each of us is like a unique flower. We differ not just in the tempo of our opening but also in the singular combination of conditions that support it. When we are able to honor and respect ourselves, sympathetic joy becomes a natural response. We can embrace as a practice having pure joy and heartfelt good wishes for ourselves in our success and for others in their successes. We can say over and over again, "May I enjoy my successes, and may they grow and increase." Then to include others, we can say, "May others enjoy their successes, and may they increase." Saying such phrases cultivates both our inner environment of respect and our joy for others' success.

Sympathetic joy is a practice not just for enjoying success. It can also be a practice for cultivating joy. We can, for example, take a few moments before going to bed to think about all the things that brought joy to us that day—a smile from a bus driver, a bird flying overhead, all those small moments. We can also take time to appreciate the efforts we have made through the day. Gratitude is a powerful way of cultivating joy.

My first spiritual practice was training with a part Native American medicine woman named Evelyn Eaton. I was lucky enough to spend some time living with her and to take part in different kinds of rituals. When I was leaving to go home, I asked her what I should do. She replied, "Every night go outside—no matter what the weather is—and spend twenty minutes giving thanks. That is all. That is your practice." I said to her, "Well, that is hard for me. I do not feel like I have enough things to give thanks for." She looked at me and said, "You have a car?" "Yes." "Give thanks for the car. Does your car have four wheels? Give thanks that your car has four wheels and a steering wheel, that it can get you places, that at least it does not leak." And so she went on, and we found twenty minutes' worth of things to be thankful for. This practice was not at all different from the Buddhist practice of cultivating joy. — AW

We can listen to music, play music, or go dancing. We can practice sympathetic joy, as we do mindfulness, in such ordinary daily activities as brushing our teeth. Some of us may have habitual patterns when we brush our teeth, such as wandering into another room or looking out the window, because we find the activity so boring. But as Thich Nhat Hanh has so eloquently asked, "Do you realize what a gift it is to have teeth?" When we contemplate what our lives would be like without teeth—and that losing their teeth may have limited the life span of very early peoples—we can begin to take joy in having teeth and even in brushing them.

All these forms of sympathetic joy open our heart connection to ourselves and others. But our lives are not always filled with successes and joy. It is the divine abode of equanimity that enables us, with peace and open-heartedness, to live life as it comes.

....

Equanimity

Equanimity asks us to open to everything with the understanding that this is how it *is*, without judgment, without grasping, without aversion. Equanimity is quite simply the absence of both grasping and aversion—it is a deep acceptance of how things are.

The Buddha said that all human beings are blown by the winds of fortune and misfortune, characterized as the eight vicissitudes: pleasure and pain, gain and loss, praise and blame, and fame and disrepute. We go through all sorts of changes in our lives. Sometimes we may be popular, but sometimes we may be blamed and turned into a scapegoat. Sometimes we may enjoy material success, but sometimes we may experience material misfortune. According to the Buddha, such ups and downs are nothing more than natural changes, and we will all go through them. But in American culture we are taught that it is acceptable to experience only some of them. It is all right to become famous and to experience pleasure and gain. It is not all right to experience pain, loss, or disrepute.

The constant changes in our lives sometimes are as small as an unexpectedly bad meal at our favorite restaurant, sometimes as great as the loss of a loved one or a career. But they come. When we can acknowledge that these changes are part of the universal law of life without trying to hold on to or push away any of them, we can come to a deep equanimity.

We can cultivate equanimity in the same way that we practice lovingkindness and sympathetic joy—by bringing into our practice and repeating phrases such as "May I have peace amid the changes in my life, and may I have peace amid the changes in others' lives." During particularly disruptive times, you may want to make equanimity your main practice.

Equanimity is the strength to stay open-hearted and stable through changing conditions. A mother devotes her life to raising her child, but when her child becomes old enough to leave home, the mother has to let go. She does not throw her child out into the street—she lets her child move on into the world and continues to love and cherish him or her.

Indifference is the near enemy of equanimity. Indifference is the expression of a closed-down heart that meets changes with defensiveness and no caring. A habitual response to change is to shut down and to try to protect ourselves, but we might also, in the midst of change, experience moments when our hearts stretch to include the whole world—all the joys and all the sorrows—with no barriers. At such times we experience ease and peace because everything is held just as it is, with no judgment, desire, or fuzziness. Equanimity is based on this clarity of wisdom and the open-heartedness of lovingkindness.

The intention expressed in phrases such as "May I have peace amid changes" is based on the understanding of karma (see pages 85–88), the knowledge that the misfortunes we experience come about through the fruition of particular conditions. Our situation is not due to just bad luck; what happens to us and to all beings is subject to the universal law of causality.

A traditional Buddhist story well illustrates the extremes of both equanimity and mindfulness in the moment. One day a man goes for a walk along a cliff high above a turbulent sea. Strolling along, enjoying the sunny day and the sound of waves crashing against the rocks, he suddenly feels the earth give way and finds himself sliding down the cliffside to certain death on the jagged rocks below. He sees a root exposed by the slide and grasps it with one hand to stop his fall. As he is hanging there, he hears a scurrying sound above him and looks up. And what does he see? A little field mouse is starting to gnaw at the root that is keeping him from plunging onto the rocks. As the man looks at the mouse, he notices to his right an exquisite wild strawberry. He stretches his free hand as far as he can, plucks the strawberry, and places it in his mouth just as the root gives way. As he starts to fall, he is fully present to the taste of the strawberry and says to himself, "Ah, what a delight!"

The Buddha and all the teachers who have followed in this lineage have spoken of our worthiness in deserving the deepest lovingkindness, compassion, sympathetic joy, and equanimity. They have stressed consistently that self-judgment and self-negation, or shame, are never ever justified. The intentional cultivation of the divine abodes heals our tendency to distort who we truly are. For a while we may feel as though we are saying lovingkindness or equanimity phrases as some kind of rote exercise—somewhat like misbehaving in school and having to write out a hundred times "I will not talk in class" but knowing that we will talk again. But over time—and it may take years—we come to see that our sense of unworthiness is just an idea inherited from our past and simply is not true. Such ideas are not an accurate reflection of who we are. The divine abodes invite us to love and respect ourselves even when we are imperfect and make mistakes. The cultivation of mindfulness and the divine abodes toward ourselves and others deeply transforms our lives, bringing us freedom and joy within each moment.

Generosity

Generosity, or *dana* (Sanskrit and Pali), in many ways is an appropriate summation of the Buddha's teaching. Generosity is supported by the belief that freedom is possible and that it does not depend on having things, keeping things, and holding on to things. Like the other practices in this path, generosity is supported by faith in the practice of giving, faith in the teachings of the Buddha, and faith in the support of the Sangha. The benefits of generosity are determined not only by our own act of giving but also by the purity of those to whom we give.

The Buddha said that if we knew the value of giving, we would not take a single meal without sharing it with others. Whenever he went into a new community to teach, his first topic was generosity. In his discourses he talked about the benefits of giving, and he said that one who gives earns the love of others, cements friendship, wins the sympathy of others, lives with a good reputation, can attend any gathering with confidence and dignity, wins popularity, and is the person with whom people of noble character want to associate.

While I was a resident teacher at Insight Meditation Society, a staff person who had just been diagnosed with breast cancer came to see me. As she was leaving, my eyes lighted on my favorite teddy bear, which I had carried around for many years, sitting on my pillow, close to the door. In a moment of spontaneous generosity, I gave it to this woman. She was touched by the gift, but I think the experience was even more profound for me because, in the giving, a special relationship was created between us. She went away for surgery and recuperation and I never saw her again, but I thought of her often because I gave her something I treasured so much. It bonded us. — AW

Giving is like a boomerang: what we give comes back to reward us many times over. We cannot lose by being generous.

True generosity is illustrated in the story of an old Zen monk who lived very simply in a hut. One night he was watching the moon through the window, sitting so still that a thief coming to steal from him did not see him. When the robber looked around, the old monk said, "Take my clothes; they are all I have. I'm so sorry. I wish I had more to give you." The monk looked at the moon shining through the open door and window and said, "I wish I had the moon that you could leave with that in your arms." The old monk understood that sharing and giving lift the heart into joy. Whatever we share and give away, we never lose because no one can take joy or generosity or lovingkindness from someone. When we give, these qualities keep on growing.

Any time we grip tightly, we experience contraction and

separation. Joseph Goldstein tells what happened to some monkeys who would not let go. A community of farmers whose crops were being eaten by wild monkeys set a special kind of trap. They hollowed out coconuts with a small hole at the top, just large enough for a monkey to put its hand through to grasp a delicacy inside, then tied these coconuts around their property. A monkey would put its hand through the hole, grasp the delicacy, but be unable to pull its hand out without letting go of the morsel. Even when farmers captured them, the monkeys would not let go. Whenever we are holding on tightly, suffering, like the farmers, is coming down the path.

We can lift our spirits by contemplating all the acts of generosity that are happening right in this moment—for example, a mother feeding her child, donors giving blood or organs that others might survive, people smiling at others in shops and buses and trains, motorists stopping to let pedestrians go by, people chanting and saying blessings and prayers for all beings. Thinking of the countless acts of generosity occurring somewhere in the world at every moment can not only warm our heart but also support our own commitment to cultivate generosity.

DANA

The Buddha said that the greatest gift we could give others is the gift of practicing the Dharma. Within this spirit, in the Theravada tradition, teachers—both ordained and lay—have always shared the teachings of the Dharma and their own practice without charging any fees. If students or an audience have felt moved, they have given *dana* ("gift" in Pali and Sanskrit)—food, medicine, and robes to monks; money or other things to lay teachers—to enable teachers to continue to practice and to teach the Dharma. In this tradition of freely giving the teachings, teachers and the monastic community have survived for 2,500 years through *dana.*

It has been one of the most beautiful parts of the Theravada tradition for me as a teacher to continually share the Dharma freely. That does not mean that there have not been times when I've felt insecure because I did not have any money. But the practice of dana *has been an extraordinary practice for me because over and over again it has supported me to let go and to give.* — AW

Our Lives as Practice

It is difficult to turn off our automatic pilot and live our lives mindfully—if it were easy, we would all be enlightened already. Although it is not easy, it is possible, and our degree of awareness depends on the amount of effort and diligence we bring to our practice. That is all.

Students of Insight Meditation often have a sense that formal meditation—such as walking meditation or meditation on the divine abodes—is The Practice and that all things outside of it are not. We assume that the times when we are standing under the shower, opening a door, and going from the sink to the toilet and the toilet to the sink are not meditations, but that is absolutely not true. They can all become meditations.

Just as in meditation we can repeatedly turn from thinking and focus again on our breath, so too can we repeatedly return from mindless moments in our daily life to awareness of what we are doing. There are many ways to remember to be present. Thich Nhat Hanh, on his retreats and at his Plum Village center in France, for decades has been giving people training in integrating awareness practice into their daily lives by sounding mindfulness bells throughout the day. Each of us has many opportunities every day to extend this practice into our lives.

- Make a list of all the sounds you can use as mindfulness bells in your life. They might include a clock chiming on the quarter-hour or hour, the telephone, the doorbell, the timer on the stove or microwave oven, even—if you live in an urban area or commute by car—the sounds of car horns and sirens.
- Each time one of your "mindfulness bells" sounds, pause, take three breaths, and connect with yourself and what you are doing.

Because some of these sounds, such as the clock, are predictable, this practice can be an especially helpful way to bring mindfulness into your daily life all day long.

I have a friend who has a timer on her watch that beeps every hour. When she hears the beep, she remembers to send metta to all beings. We have a clock at home that chimes London's Big Ben every hour. When the chimes sound, I stop what I am doing and take a moment to breathe or just become aware of what is happening inside of me. I love this clock. It is such a great reminder and mirror of my mind states. Sometimes I hear it and watch myself resist stopping and stop only at the last chime. Then I know I am rushing. Sometimes I stop, and my breath is so tight I am really surprised. Sometimes I stop, and I love the break of letting go and allowing things to come to balance. — AW

We all need to eat, and eating is another wonderful way to reconnect with ourselves.

My partner and I have found it tremendously helpful to take some mindful moments of silence before we eat. After sitting in silence, we sometimes say a blessing, such as:

"We give thanks to the life of these plants and also to the animals [if you eat meat] for giving their life to us so that we might live. We give thanks to the earth, the sun, the waters, and the farmers who planted and harvested the food and those who transported it to workers in the shops. We give thanks for the tremendous amount of energy that is gone into bringing this food to us. To those who prepared the food for us, we give our gratitude. May all beings have enough to eat."

Sometimes our guests are a little uncomfortable with the silence and blessing, but the feelings generated are very warm and loving. Also, kids love saying blessings, and that is a wonderful way to involve children in the process. — AW

Slowly over time we can expand these little practices to cover more of the things we do in our daily life. The critical thing is to repeatedly find the places where the door is open a little bit already so we can come through into connection with ourselves. There is no one right way. The way is whatever works for each of us, and it is different according to our conditions and what we like and what we do not like. It is important to know what those conditions are. Some people, for example, might sit down and breathe for a few moments. Others, however, could not possibly sit down to meditate—for them, the solution might be to drop everything and go for a walk, connecting to the sensations of movement. Still others might take a bit of time to sing some songs—perhaps in the shower.

It is helpful to find the time to meditate, but that time does not have to be the only time we practice. Each moment that we can remember to connect to what we are doing, we are purifying ourselves—whether it is in a moment of speaking, picking up a pen to write something, or walking up the stairs. Each moment we remember, we are on the path to freedom.

Those moments of awareness may feel very tiny, and we may feel as if nothing is happening, but that is not true. Each moment counts. The law of karma says that each moment actually creates the conditions for the fruition of that moment, and the next, and the next. It is like the classic image of a bucket under a leaky faucet. You have the drip, drip. Each drip is a tiny amount—not a big deal. But if you leave your bucket under the faucet for a few days, it gets full. Training our minds to remember, moment by moment, serves our happiness. It is not just a technique—mindfulness is actually a practice of freedom and happiness.

Exercise: Daily Practice

You can strengthen your capacity to be mindful in your daily life by choosing some specific prompts.

Pick one simple everyday action, and use this one action in particular to try to train yourself to remember what you are doing. It might be walking upstairs, which can bring you back to yourself through feeling the effort of thigh muscles lifting the body. It might be turning the knob to the bedroom door. It might be riding in an elevator at work, or opening the car door, or just sitting there while the car warms up.

Write yourself a note in your diary, and give yourself cues that you can easily see. Write a cue on your bathroom mirror, or tie a note on your car door or your bedroom doorknob or the banister of your stairs—"May I remember to remember that I'm walking up these stairs." And every time you take that action, remember to do it mindfully.

When you feel that you have become very mindful at walking up the stairs, expand the practice to one more action. Now you are walking up the stairs and you are also turning the knob of your bedroom door.

When you feel you are ready, add another prompt to your list.

10. Our Guides and Supports: Teachers, Sanghas, and Retreats

I would like to honor my lineage and my root teacher, Ruth Denison. I would like to honor her teacher, the Burmese master U Ba Khin, who died in 1971. U Ba Khin, a layperson who became the accountant general of Burma as well as being a remarkable teacher, founded the International Meditation Center in Rangoon, where he was one of the first teachers to teach Western laywomen. U Ba Khin's best-known students are Ruth Denison and S. N. Goenka. His teacher, Saya Thetgyi, was a farmer supported to teach by a famous Burmese scholar and monk. Although many monks and nuns were initially skeptical because Saya Thetgyi had no formal education, they soon realized the depth of his practice and came to hear his discourses.

And so it has gone, teacher to student to teacher, all the way back to the Buddha. — AW

....

Dharma Teachers

Our Dharma teachers, for many of us, are like mothers—so we honor them for "birthing" us into our Dharma beings, into a world that is fundamentally different and profoundly healing.

Without teachers—both those who are ordained and those who are not—the Dharma would not be available to us today. Their practice, purity, wisdom, and dedication have kept the Dharma vibrant and uncontaminated over successive generations for 2,500 years.

In most Buddhist traditions, Dharma teachers are heirs of particular lineages. Lineage is one way to foster the pure transmission of the Buddha's teachings from a teacher to a pupil who becomes a teacher to another pupil. Lineage is the acknowledgment by a teacher that a student truly understands and can teach the Dharma. Thus, teachers in formal lineages have received acknowledgment and empowerment to transmit the Dharma. In this way, the Dharma has been communicated with a degree of purity that is astounding, given how old it is.

The formal acknowledgment that a student receives is one kind of transmission, but we can receive transmissions of the Dharma in many ways. Sometimes it happens as we listen to the formal teachings of the Dharma and our mind opens to the truth. At other times, hearing a birdsong can trigger awakening. In that moment, we touch the truth and experience a kind of a transmission. Experiencing truth and beauty can happen within all religions and in many other circumstances, and it is important to acknowledge all our sources of transmission.

CHOOSING A TEACHER

In the Tibetan and Zen traditions, one of the main constituents of the student-teacher relationship is devotion—the student sees the teacher as the perfect embodiment of the Dharma. Through devotion to that purity, the Dharma is transmitted.

In the Theravada tradition, however, the emphasis is not so much on the teacher-student relationship as on our own practice. A teacher is simply a guide, and a *kalyanamitta* ("spiritual friend" in Pali). There is not very much ritual in the relationship. We are not required to vow devotion to teachers or commit ourselves to a lifelong—or lives-long—relationship to any one teacher. There is no need "to submit to the authority of the teacher" in the sense of never disagreeing. In the Theravada tradition, there has always been space to challenge, to question, and to know that in the end finding the truth is our own responsibility. This does not mean that we cannot receive our teachers' guidance with an open heart.

After sitting with different teachers, most students find it useful to sit repeatedly with one or two so that there will be continuity in guidance. One possibility is for students who live in an area with a center to develop an ongoing relationship with a teacher at that center. Another place where students connect with Insight Meditation teachers is on retreat (see pages 168–175). There, in addition to hearing Dharma talks, students have time to meet with teachers either in groups or in individual interviews, where personal guidance can be given. What is important in choosing a teacher is to find someone you feel safe with, someone you feel comfortable with, someone whose teachings resonate within you. No one teacher is inherently better than another, but some teachers say things in a way that makes more sense: You can hear them.

When you think you want to study with a particular teacher, it is important not to dive in all at once. Take some time to ensure that you have chosen well. Notice how the teacher behaves. Does this teacher live within the guidelines of the Five Precepts (see pages 102–110)? How does this teacher answer questions? Can you personally spend time with this teacher?

I decided to spend quite a bit of time with my teacher in the beginning. I followed her around like a groupie, going from retreat to retreat, and I also spent quite a lot of time at her center. Having that kind of contact and having a close personal relationship with her provided me with the conditions I needed to grow. That is not always true for everyone. For some people, a formal relationship during retreats is fine. Also, after I had been grounded in my practice for a long while, there were stretches when I did self-retreats for years and did not work with any teacher at all. So our relationship with a teacher or not working with one comes about through understanding what we need at different stages of our spiritual growth. — AW

In his discourses the Buddha often said that associating with good friends who are practicing the Dharma becomes one of the conditions for the arising of mindfulness, faith, and many of the other skillful qualities. Our teachers are such good friends. Even—or perhaps especially—when they are not giving Dharma talks but are just being, their actions can be models and inspiration for us.

Recently I went to a retreat at Ruth's center, and I went with her to visit her husband, who has advanced Alzheimer's. She has been his primary caretaker for many difficult years now. I was struck by how patient and loving she was with him, and I said that to her. She replied, "Darling, what else should I be?" — AW

Note: Although it has not happened as often in the Theravada tradition as in others, teachers have occasionally achieved great wisdom without integrating it on the personality level, and they have not always behaved ethically toward some students or the sangha. If you ever have a challenging experience with a Theravada teacher, you can communicate with the ethics council at Spirit Rock Meditation Center (see page 218 for the address). This council was created to support Insight Meditation teachers to uphold purity of conduct in relationship to students. Most teachers, however, are deeply committed to ethical conduct.

....

Sangha Today

Whether our sangha is at a center or in our own living room, students of Insight Meditation are a powerful support and example for each other. We become each other's mindfulness mirror. When we forget, we are reminded. When we have remembered, we become the reminders for others. Our presence raises their energy level, and their presence buttresses our commitment to continue to practice. In a sangha we become a community that supports the best of ourselves and also supports the abandoning of the worst of ourselves. What greater gift can we give each other than that?

On Thich Nhat Hanh's retreats at Plum Village, France, when the lunch bell rings, long lines form, and laypeople like me are at

the end, after monks and nuns. While I was there, sometimes
150 or 200 people were ahead of me, and what food was left was
cold by the time laypeople served themselves. I decided to just
continue sitting when the bell rang and to come to the dining hall
when the line was almost finished. There wasn't much point in
being there early.

But that plan was not to be. In almost every Dharma talk,
Thây [Thich Nhat Hanh] mentioned that we cannot follow this
path alone—we need to be part of a sangha that is practicing.
And for a sangha to practice, we have to turn up, not just for our-
selves but for everyone else as well. When a community of people
sit and walk and eat and breathe together in mindfulness, there
is holiness. One day Thây specifically said that we need to turn
up together when the bell rings for lunch. When we are mindfully
standing in line, we are an inspiration for those who may have
forgotten to be mindful. His words really touched me, and I then
made it a formal practice, when the lunch bell rang, to go and be
mindful of how I was standing, of my breathing, and of the mind
of desire, wanting to get to the table before the food ran out or got
cold. After a while my commitment to being there and being pres-
ent opened my heart so that my contraction around the food dis-
appeared. — AW

Sangha is the Third Refuge (see page 8), the safe community that is transmitting and living the Buddha's teachings. Traditionally, sangha was seen as the ordained community that
was fully awakened. Today the word *sangha* extends to those
lay communities that practice as well.

Because our practice is enormously enhanced by the
support of a sangha, it is helpful to find a group to sit with.
The resource listings in chapter 15 can assist you to find a
group nearby. If you do not live close to a center, try calling

the nearest one, because most maintain lists of sitting groups in their area.

In urban areas you can usually find other people who are practicing Insight Meditation, but if you live in a small town, consider starting your own group. You can gather with acquaintances who may not be on exactly the same spiritual path as you are, but you can still support each other's practice simply by your presence in the same room. Some groups meet successfully in private homes, often moving the meeting place from home to home, while others find it best to meet in a "neutral" space such as a library or community room. In any case, groups often have found it most useful to rotate leadership. If you do start a sitting group, it is very important to attend some retreats at a retreat center, too, especially so that you will have the opportunity for formal instruction and work with a teacher. Attending retreats can be a most effective way to support the opening of our heart and mind.

Going on Retreats

When you want to learn a skill, you go to a class. You go to a yoga class to learn yoga, to a dance class to learn ballet, to a music class to learn an instrument. In the same way, there is no better opportunity to develop our meditation skills than to go to a meditation class or retreat, which at many centers is literally called a course.

The Western teachers who began the first Insight Meditation centers in the United States wanted to give their students the opportunity to practice within a special setting, as people do in Asia, but without all the rituals and formal elements that are so much part of Asian monastic life. What they retained

Retreat Jobs This retreatant at Spirit Rock helps wash dishes, one of the tasks retreatants volunteer for in order to keep the cost of retreats low.

was an atmosphere where practice is supported by structured conditions such as silence and by the efforts of others.

A retreat is a temporary community where everyone is committed to the same thing, which produces extraordinary energy and support. When you are feeling numb and see others walking mindfully, it helps you to walk mindfully. If you do not think you can sit still for another minute but everyone else in the room does, that helps you to sit still. Just the energy of all those minds meditating changes the environment so that everyone's mindfulness can become stronger.

A retreat is also a community in which everyone is practicing the same morality—no one is robbed, mugged, or raped on a retreat. Retreats thus create temporary spaces that are safe and healing, and because we do not have the demands of work or families, it becomes easier to go inside ourselves. On retreat we can connect more easily with ourselves than when we are practicing alone, so going on retreat is a critical ingredient for most of us on this path.

Although retreats vary from center to center, most retreats have many common elements. They often start on Friday evenings and last for a weekend, a week, ten days, or longer. When

Entering the Meditation Hall
Before entering the meditation hall, retreatants place their shoes on the spaces provided.

students arrive, they are assigned to a room or dormitory and usually sign up for a daily task such as chopping vegetables, washing dishes, vacuuming hallways, or cleaning a bathroom. Taking care of these chores is an exercise in mindfulness and also keeps the cost of the retreat as low as possible. New arrivals often then remove their shoes and go into the meditation hall to select the place where they will sit for the duration of the retreat. Even before retreats begin, silence is maintained in the meditation hall. Some students bring their own cushions; large centers tend to have a number of cushions and benches available for retreatants. There are also usually some chairs set up around the sides of the room for those who prefer to meditate in chairs. Students leave a cushion, shawl, or other personal item on the spot they have chosen so that others will know that the place is taken.

Unless another retreat is already in progress, silence outside the meditation hall usually does not begin until the first evening's Dharma talk. This enables students to greet old friends, talk as they get settled in their sleeping area, and get to know others during the light supper served.

A SAMPLE RETREAT SCHEDULE

After the first evening, a retreat usually follows a daily schedule something like this:

5:15 A.M.:	Wake-up bell
5:45 A.M.:	First sitting
6:30 A.M.:	Breakfast
7:30 A.M.:	Work period
9:00 A.M.:	Sitting, instructions
9:45 A.M.:	Walking
10:00 A.M.:	Sitting
10:45 A.M.:	Walking
11:30 A.M.:	Sitting
12:15 P.M.:	Lunch, rest
2:15 P.M.:	Walking
2:45 P.M.:	Sitting
3:30 P.M.:	Walking
4:15 P.M.:	Sitting
5:00 P.M.:	Walking
5:30 P.M.:	Light supper
6:30 P.M.:	Sitting
7:00 P.M.:	Walking
7:30 P.M.:	Dharma talk
8:30 P.M.:	Walking
9:00 P.M.:	Sitting
9:30 P.M.:	Late tea, sleep, or more practice

Alternative schedules may start a little later, perhaps at 6:30 A.M., and may also include question-and-answer periods and guided-movement sessions. If this schedule looks impossible, do not worry. At Insight Meditation retreats, there is always support for you to find your own rhythm and what works best for you. Some students find surrendering to the form of the schedule helpful, but others find that they need to create their own rhythm—sometimes taking longer walks, sometimes sitting for much less time than the schedule indicates. One schedule is not better than another. What is most important to find out is what works for you.

DHARMA TALKS

Daily *Dharma talks* are given by teachers on topics from the Buddha's teachings and also from their own or others' experiences of living a life of practice. The first evening, students are usually invited to take the Three Refuges (pages 5–8) after they are described, and then the Five Precepts (pages 102–110), which is the code of conduct for the retreat. Depending upon the length of the retreat and whether it has a special focus, Dharma talks may discuss difficulties in meditation, or the hindrances (pages 33–50), the Four Noble Truths (chapter 5), the divine abodes (chapter 9), or any number of other topics, such as wisdom (chapter 6) and the seven factors of enlightenment (pages 130–132).

MEDITATION PERIODS

Periods of sitting usually alternate with periods of walking meditation throughout the day. Sitting is generally done in the meditation hall, but it can also be done in one's own bedroom, outside, or in any quiet place at the center. Often specific meditation instructions in mindfulness are given during the first sitting period after breakfast either the first day or every day. Instructions in lovingkindness meditation and movement meditation are also sometimes given.

The difficulties encountered in meditation—especially

Walking Meditation
This hall at the Insight Meditation Society is dedicated to indoor walking meditation. Meditators walk back and forth across the room at their own pace, similar to the way retreatants walk outdoors (page 25).

drowsiness—seem to be strong during the first several days of a retreat. For many students, suddenly shifting from an active life with a great deal of stimulation to sitting in a silent room with eyes closed is a formula for instant sleepiness. It passes, and the suggestions on pages 42–43 can help the transition.

Where walking meditation is done depends upon where the retreat is held. Most centers have walking rooms in which students walk for a distance of twenty to thirty feet, turn around, and walk back, doing walking meditation as described in chapter 2. If weather permits, many students prefer to walk outside, choosing their "lane" and staying within it. Sometimes, especially if they are feeling sleepy, students take a fast walk to raise their energy. It is not advisable to do the three-speed walking on a public sidewalk or roadway.

Depending upon the length of a retreat, either on the last evening or on the last morning there usually is a session during which retreatants are given instructions for cleaning their rooms, and rides home are coordinated. Someone will give a talk about *dana* (see pages 156–157). Because the Buddha's teachings are priceless, Theravada teachers never charge for their teachings—the retreat fees cover only the costs of running the retreat. Instead, a basket is placed near the exit so that students who wish to make donations to support the teachers and the continuation of these teachings can do so. Because of the generosity of those who came before us, the teachings have been freely given for nearly three millennia.

Before my first retreat, I knew about dana *and worried about how much to contribute. Was there some magic formula related to the cost of the retreat, whose price covers only the expense of housing and feeding students? I waited till the last moment, then, deeply moved by the closing Dharma talk, I wrote a check for more than I could really afford at the time. Since then, I've always made my check out before a retreat. I've asked myself what the Dharma is worth to me and what I can afford to pay for its continuation. I'm not paying this teacher for this retreat. Whether I like what any given teacher does on a retreat, I'm giving as much as I reasonably can to support the Dharma for the future.* — JS

Although some people prefer to determine ahead of time what they can afford to give, others find it helpful to allow the mindfulness and generosity that have been cultivated to express themselves at the end of the retreat in whatever amount seems right.

Near the end of a retreat, there also often is some sort of sharing session, breaking silence so that everyone can share their experience during the retreat. Many retreats end with everyone doing *metta* (see pages 139–143).

What Kind of Retreat?

Insight Meditation retreats may last for one day or for months. They may be residential or nonresidential. They may be held at an established Insight Meditation retreat center, or they may be held in rented space at a suitable facility. Where you go and how long you stay depend upon your own needs and the circumstances of your life.

One-day retreats often focus on a specific topic, such as working with chronic illness or generosity. Longer retreats most often are Insight Meditation retreats, but *metta* retreats are increasingly popular. Retreats for families, women, men, gays and lesbians, young people, and old (experienced) students are offered frequently in many places throughout the United States and Europe.

INSIGHT MEDITATION CENTERS

Some retreat centers are large and beautifully situated in spacious rural settings. Others occupy little more than a Web site on the Internet and an answering service and rely entirely on rented space for their retreats.

The first major Insight Meditation center in the United States was the Insight Meditation Society (IMS) in Barre, Massachusetts, founded in 1975 by Joseph Goldstein, Sharon Salzberg, Jack Kornfield, and visionary colleagues such as Jacqueline Mandell, who joined the staff a year later. Located in lovely wooded hills in central Massachusetts, IMS occupies a former Christian monastery, whose basement bowling alley

Insight Meditation Society   This center, in Barre, Massachusetts, was the first Insight Meditation center founded in the United States. Retreatants enter the main building, which houses the office, dining room, teacher interview rooms, and staff sleeping quarters. The center structure is the walking meditation room shown on page 173, and the building farthest to the left is the meditation hall.

has become a favorite spot for walking meditation. The retreats, ranging from two days to three months, accommodate about a hundred students and are taught by both IMS teachers and visiting teachers from throughout the United States, Europe, and Asia. In 1990 the Insight Meditation Society founded the Barre Center for Buddhist Studies, which brings together scholars and practitioners from all Buddhist traditions to explore the relationship between study and practice. IMS is also developing a long-term practice center, a forest refuge, in woods adjoining the main center.

A very different center is the Bhavana Society's forest monastery in High View, West Virginia, founded in 1983 by Sri Lankan teacher Venerable Henepola Gunaratana. Established in the Asian forest tradition, the center has modest facilities, including huts (*kutis*), and in the late 1990s it completed a beautiful new meditation hall. It offers weekend and ten-day retreats, has ceremonies for traditional Buddhist holidays, and ordains monks and nuns who wish to live and train there as monastics.

A number of centers have been founded in California. A striking setting is the home of the Dhamma Dena Desert Vipassana Center in Joshua Tree. Founded in 1977 by Ruth Denison, the center offers retreats from two days to three weeks, primarily during the cooler months of the year. The unassuming accommodations and the emphasis on the beautiful desert surroundings encourage retreatants to integrate their practice with the setting. This center is renowned for the creative and varied practices of cultivating mindfulness and guided movement and for the unique teachings of Denison.

Dhamma Dena Desert Meditation Center At Ruth Denison's center, near Joshua Tree, California, retreatants are exposed to such unique meditation experiences as doing movement meditation led by Denison in a nearby hot spring.

Kuti Ajahn Amaro at the small hut *(kuti)* where he lives at
Abhayagiri Buddhist Monastery.

The Abhayagiri Buddhist Monastery, in Redwood Valley,
California, like the Bhavana Society in West Virginia, continues
the Asian forest tradition. Founded by British monk Ajahn
Amaro in 1996, it is in the Thai tradition of Achaan Chah, via
the Amaravati Monastery in England. Abhayagiri has extremely
humble housing and a meditation room for those training
there for ordination. No public retreats are held at the monastery, but Ajahn Amaro does teach retreats in facilities else-
where in California and throughout the United States. Some
Abhayagiri programs, including traditional Theravada ceremonies and weekly Dharma talks, are open to visitors. Visiting
monks and nuns from the English forest monasteries also teach
at Insight Meditation centers; their retreats give particular
insight into monastic practice.

Spirit Rock Meditation Center, originally called Insight
Meditation Society West, was founded in 1981 by Jack Korn-

field, Jamie Baraz, Sylvia Boorstein, Anna Douglas, Julie Wester, and Howie Cohn. The newest buildings here were finished in 1998, creating a graceful retreat "village" in the hills of Marin County, California. Spirit Rock offers remarkably varied courses that last from one day to eight weeks, taught by the Spirit Rock Teacher Collective and visiting teachers.

Throughout the United States, there is also a growing number of nonresidential retreat centers, such as the Cambridge (Massachusetts) Insight Meditation Center, founded by Larry Rosenberg; Dhamma Dena Meditation Center in Northampton, Massachusetts, founded by Arinna Weisman; New York Insight, founded by a group of IMS students living in New York City; the Lesbian Buddhist Sangha, in Oakland, California, founded by Carol Newhouse under the umbrella of the Women's Dharma Foundation and the Women's Dharma Group of Sebastopol; the Taos (New Mexico) Mountain

Spirit Rock Meditation Center   The meditation hall is nestled in the beautiful hills of Marin County, California.

Dhamma Dena Meditation Center in Northampton, Massachusetts
Arinna Weisman (left), founder of this nonresidental center, is joined by Joseph Goldstein and Ruth Denison for a fundraiser in support of the new center.

Sangha, founded by Marcia Rose; and the Seattle Insight Meditation Society, founded by Rodney Smith. These centers offer ongoing classes, nonresidential and residential retreats, drop-in sittings, and contact with teachers.

These are just a few of the many Insight Meditation centers in the United States, and sitting groups are growing in number in all parts of the country. Many of these centers can be found in the list in chapter 15. The most comprehensive and current list of Insight Meditation retreats can be found in the journal *Inquiring Mind* (see page 220).

11. Frequently Asked Questions

Are you Buddhists?

It is not considered important to label oneself a Buddhist. Many people, including teachers of the Dharma, do not call themselves Buddhists, so that label is not a clear reflection of whether a person lives by the Buddha's teachings. What is important is to understand the nature of suffering and what brings liberation from it. We both personally call ourselves Buddhists because the teachings have been so central in our lives and we each have undergone such profound transformations because of them. The Buddha probably would consider it more important to be a *buddha*—an awakened one—than to call oneself a Buddhist. There is a Zen expression "If you see a Buddha walking down the road, kill him." This expression calls us to challenge the phenomenon in which some people build an identity as a "Buddhist" but at the same time forget the practice of awakening.

How does Insight Meditation, or Vipassana, differ from other major traditions?

Theravada ("Teaching of the Elders"), which includes Insight Meditation or Vipassana practice, is the oldest tradition in Buddhism. It evolved from the teachings of the Buddha as collected in the *Pali canon*. After the Second Council, during the fourth century B.C.E., splinter groups began to form, one of which eventually became the powerful Mahayana ("Greater Vehicle") tradition. It was this group that gave the label *Hinayana* ("Lesser Vehicle") to Theravada Buddhism. In a sense, the Mahayana Buddhists were the "young Turks" of early Buddhism, broadening the base of practice and texts to accommodate a diversity of peoples as Buddhism spread through the Northern Transmission (see pages 62–63). Today, the Zen and Tibetan schools are the largest Mahayana traditions.

All Buddhist traditions understand suffering and the fact that suffering can be transformed. All understand that we can be liberated from our delusions. But the paths to awakening manifest in very different ways, not only from one tradition to another but even within the same stream. Tibetan and Zen traditions, for example, have many more formal elements and fixed rituals than Insight Meditation does. Some Tibetan traditions rely heavily on prostrations and visualization, which are not generally used in Insight Meditation. Prostrations are also practiced, though less frequently, in Zen traditions, which emphasize posture and formal rituals that are used as mindfulness practice.

In some schools of Zen, *koans*—teaching puzzles and stories such as "Kill the Buddha"—are used to free the mind; Insight Meditation practice is based on the Four Foundations of Mindfulness (see pages 120–130). Similarly, Mahayana traditions rely heavily on *sutras*, or discourses, that were "discovered" in hidden realms several hundred years later than the Pali canon, while Insight Meditation is based on the original Pali canon.

There are several other differences in emphasis. First, where Insight Meditation stresses nonharming and working for the benefit of all beings, Mahayana Buddhism focuses on the ideal of the *bodhisattva*, a being who postpones Nirvana in order to liberate all other beings. Another major difference is in the role of the teacher. In Tibetan and Zen practices, the teacher is seen as the living embodiment of the Dharma, and devotion becomes a key component in the transmission of the Dharma. By contrast, the Insight Meditation teacher is seen as a spiritual adviser and friend, and the emphasis is more on the student's own practice.

It is important to note that many different traditions exist within Theravada Buddhism, depending upon the country of origination. Sri Lankan, Thai, Vietnamese, Burmese, Indian, and American all differ from each other. Further, even several students who had the same teacher may manifest the Dharma differently, as is true, for example, for Ruth Denison and S. N. Goenka, both of whom trained with Burmese master U Ba Khin. This diversity among teachers greatly enriches the teachings.

What is the role of monasteries in Theravada Buddhism?

Men and women in many places, of diverse ages and economic backgrounds, have been called to the Dharma and have made the single-purpose commitment to realizing freedom. For many, the path for realization has meant renouncing lay life—including intimate sexual relationships, earning a livelihood, and freedom in choosing a lifestyle—and they have ordained as monks and nuns. These ordained nuns and monks have

***Bhikkhu* Ordination Ceremony** At monasteries such as Abhaya-giri, monks trained in the Thai forest tradition are ordained in this traditional ceremony.

given us an incredible gift, because they have preserved the formal tradition of the teachings through their monastic institutions and education for thousands of years. It should be noted that, as in all institutions, there have been difficulties, including rampant sexism.

The monastic tradition in Asia is still strong, and a growing number of Theravada monasteries are being established in the West—though not as many as within the Zen and Tibetan traditions.

What has been the role of women in Theravada Buddhism?

In his lifetime, the Buddha took the revolutionary step of including women—both as nuns and as lay followers—into his Sangha. Later writings made some unverified claims about how this happened, but the simple fact is that some of his closest followers and greatest teachers were women, as described in Susan Murcott's excellent book, *The First Buddhist Women*. But because of sexism in all Asian institutions, the formal transmission of the Dharma was carried out by men, and in Asia the ordained women's sangha has all but died out in the Theravada tradition—which means that the formal transmission in the monastic community from woman to woman has ended there. But this does not mean that it has not taken place. Transmission has occurred not only from monks to laywomen but also from laywoman to laywoman and from laywomen to their children in family situations, even though that transmission has not been recorded. In the Zen and Tibetan traditions, laywomen teachers have been more frequently recorded and have participated—though not as fully as men for reasons of sexism—in the practice of the Dharma. In the West today, laywomen teachers in Theravada and Zen traditions have achieved positions of prominence. Some Asian monastics have predicted that a major role of Western women—ordained and lay—will be to take the Dharma back to Asian women.

What about God in Buddhism?

The Buddha, through his own direct experience, came to a place of absolutely no separation—so at peace and so open that nothing lay outside of his heart. Everything was included, with no aversion, anger, hatred, jealousy, greed, or delusion. He realized that we all can live in the same way, whether we believe in God or gods or not. That is not a critical factor for living in the teachings of the Dharma.

Do Buddhists believe that the Buddha was a god?

No. He never claimed to be a god or a messenger of a god. One of the reasons his teachings are so powerful is that he was human like all of us, so we can see what is possible for us. When we look at and pay respect to statues of the Buddha, we are actually honoring ourselves, our own Buddha-natures.

Can I be a practicing Christian or Jew and a Buddhist at the same time?

Yes. Buddhism is not religious, in the sense that it does not depend on having a particular relationship with any kind of god or God. Rather, Buddhism depends on our own intentions and ability to live in such a way that we free ourselves from all the qualities that make us feel closed-hearted or unclear. We can practice Buddhism and at the same time follow our own original religious traditions. The transformations that come through practice of the Dharma can only enhance our other religious practices if we have them.

How does Buddhist meditation differ from Christian meditation?

In Insight Meditation the term *meditation* refers to how we focus mindfulness and concentration on the direct experience of our bodies, feelings, and so on, which brings us insight into the truth of how things really are. In Christianity *meditation* usually refers to contemplation of a scriptural passage, sacred idea, or God.

Does Theravada Buddhism believe in reincarnation?

Theravada Buddhism believes that reincarnation is the collection of positive and negative forces or karma that we have created in our lives, which "jumps" once we have died into a new birth. Theravada Buddhism says that after death, this energy of "I" moves forward into the next few moments, becoming a fetus. How it manifests depends upon a complex of particular conditions, including mind states in the moment of death. The practice of the Eightfold Path begins to purify these energies and finally to literally burn them out. Once we are free of all clinging, we have a choice of whether we want to reincarnate. The historical Buddha chose to reincarnate for thousands of years, to continue to purify himself so that he could become a buddha ("awakened one"). Mahayana Buddhism stresses that bodhisattvas, people like the Dalai Lama, continue to choose to come back in order to reduce the suffering of all beings. It is important to note that many Buddhists have rich and fulfilling practices without believing in reincarnation; many see their rebirth as part of the plants and living universe rather than as a specific being.

How do teachers become teachers?
In Insight Meditation there is no certification for Dharma teachers, but in all traditions teachers have transmitted the Dharma to students, and at some point the teachers acknowledge, "You are ready to teach." In the Zen and Tibetan traditions, the recognition is accompanied by formal rituals, as it is for Theravada students practicing within a monastic situation. The Theravada lay teachers in the West who are included in the listings in *Inquiring Mind* (see page 220) have trained under a senior teacher who recognized that they have a deep enough understanding of the Dharma that they can now teach.

Are all Buddhists vegetarian?
Not necessarily. Buddhists in Thailand, Vietnam, Burma, and Sri Lanka usually do not eat meat, while in Tibet and Japan they often do. In the West some do, and some do not. When Zen master Robert Aitken was asked if he considered eating vegetables to be killing, too, he replied yes, but that cows

scream louder than cauliflowers. Whether to be a vegetarian is a decision that each person will make for herself or himself.

What is the relationship between Buddhism and psychology?
There is no formal relationship as such, but because both Buddhism and psychology explore the mind, they are close together. Both fields bring the quality of investigation into our lives in order to achieve understanding. Psychotherapy has defined its field in the contents of our mind, our stories, our emotions, and our places of turmoil. Insight Meditation stresses disengaging from story lines and situating ourselves in our awareness of them. The beauty of Buddhism is that it is a practice that can bring about freedom—a freedom that goes beyond our personal stories. The benefits of psychology are the many techniques developed to help us unravel emotional snarls that we cannot let go of and difficulties that require a systematic and guided investigation.

12. The Sangha of One World

Our sangha can include the whole living world. Walking along, we suddenly hear the trill of a bird or the laughter of a child, or we see the silhouette of a tree against the sky, and we are reminded that all of life lives with us. If we can relate to the world around us with the same open-hearted support, respect, and honesty that we have for our traditional sangha, we can all live in peace and harmony.

When we see the whole world as our sangha, the commitment to honesty challenges us to look beyond our conditioned responses to people who are different. Our yearning for unity and freedom can move us to see if the separation we feel from "others" has hardened into prejudice or social discrimination. We may feel that divisions in our communities do not have much to do with our spiritual practice—that these problems are related to politics or welfare or charity. But when we live in unity with all of life, we challenge the ways we move people out of our hearts and into categories that rob them of their uniqueness and humanity. The reason that racism and homophobia exist in American culture, for example, is that each one of us carries those beliefs inside of us. In sometimes subtle, sometimes blatant ways those beliefs get acted out and create a pattern of discrimination. Because such discrimination is culturally sanctioned, we feel that it does not harm us, but as we become more sensitive to the suffering that exists, we are moved to create the conditions of happiness for all beings.

In this world of sangha, we are each other's environment. Each wave in the ocean is independent in its formation and at the same time is inseparable from the whole. There is no such thing as a wave without the ocean. In the same way, we are inseparable from each other and are connected to the whole body of life.

13. Selected Texts

Theravada Buddhism is based on the Pali canon, the collection of the Buddha's teachings authorized by his senior disciples shortly after his death. Because of the importance of some of these discourses to many chapters in this book, we have included them; the repetitions that characterize material originally transmitted orally have been shortened. We have also included some verses from the *Dhammapada* to give a flavor of the Buddha's teachings.

....

Suttas

FOUR NOBLE TRUTHS

When the Buddha gave his first sermon at the Deer Park near Benares, he expounded the Four Noble Truths. These teachings became the foundation of the Buddha's later discourses, or suttas

(Pali; sutras in Sanskrit) and form the basis of all the Buddhist teachings that evolved later.

The venerable Sariputta said this:

"At Benares, friends, in the Deer Park at Isipatana the Tathagata [the Buddha], accomplished and fully enlightened, set rolling the matchless Wheel of the Dhamma . . . and exhibiting of the Four Noble Truths. Of what four?

"The announcing . . . and exhibiting of the noble truth of suffering . . . of the noble truth of the origin of suffering . . . of the noble truth of the cessation of suffering . . . of the noble truth of the way leading to the cessation of suffering.

"And what, friends, is the noble truth of suffering? Birth is suffering; ageing is suffering; death is suffering; sorrow, lamentation, pain, grief, and despair are suffering; not to obtain what one wants is suffering; in short, the five aggregates affected by clinging are suffering.

"And what, friends, is birth? The birth of beings into the various orders of beings, their coming to birth, precipitation [in a womb], generation, the manifestation of the aggregates, obtaining the bases for contact—this is called birth.

"And what, friends, is ageing? The ageing of beings in the various orders of beings, their old age, brokenness of teeth, greyness of hair, wrinkling of skin, decline of life, weakness of faculties—this is called ageing.

"And what, friends, is death? The passing of beings out of the various orders of beings, their passing away, dissolution, disappearance, dying, completion of time, dissolution of aggregates, laying down of the body—this is called death.

"And what, friends, is sorrow? The sorrow, sorrowing, sorrowfulness, inner sorrow, inner sorriness, of one who has encountered some misfortune or is affected by some painful state—this is called sorrow.

"And what, friends, is lamentation? The wail and lament, wailing and lamenting, bewailing and lamentation, of one who has encountered some misfortune or is affected by some painful state—this is called lamentation.

"And what, friends, is pain? Bodily pain, bodily discomfort, painful, uncomfortable feeling born of bodily contact—this is called pain.

"And what, friends, is grief? Mental pain, mental discomfort, painful, uncomfortable feeling born of mental contact—this is called grief.

"And what, friends, is despair? The trouble and despair, the tribulation and desperation, of one who has encountered some misfortune or is affected by some painful state—this is called despair.

"And what, friends, is 'not to obtain what one wants is suffering'? To beings subject to birth there comes the wish: 'Oh, that we were not subject to birth! That birth would not come to us!' But this is not to be obtained by wishing, and not to obtain what one wants is suffering. To beings subject to ageing . . . subject to sickness . . . subject to death . . . subject to sorrow, lamentation, pain, grief, and despair, there comes the wish: 'Oh, that we were not subject to sorrow, lamentation, pain, grief, and despair! That sorrow, lamentation, pain, grief, and despair would not come to us!' But this is not to be obtained by wishing, and not to obtain what one wants is suffering.

"And what, friends, are the five aggregates affected by clinging that, in short, are suffering? They are: the material form aggregate affected by clinging, the feeling aggregate affected by clinging, the perception aggregate affected by clinging, the formations aggregate affected by clinging, and the consciousness aggregate affected by clinging. These are the five aggregates affected by clinging that, in short, are suffering. This is called the noble truth of suffering.

"And what, friends, is the noble truth of the origin of suffering? It is craving, which brings renewal of being, is accompanied by delight and lust, and delights in this and that; that is, craving for sensual pleasures, craving for being, and craving for non-being. This is called the noble truth of the origin of suffering.

"And what, friends, is the noble truth of the cessation of suffering? It is the remainderless fading away and ceasing, the giving up, relinquishing, letting go, and rejecting of that same craving. This is called the noble truth of the cessation of suffering.

"And what, friends, is the noble truth of the way leading to the cessation of suffering? It is just this Noble Eightfold Path; that is, right view, right intention, right speech, right action, right livelihood, right effort, right mindfulness, and right concentration.

"And what, friends, is right view? Knowledge of suffering, knowledge of the origin of suffering, knowledge of the cessation of suffering, and knowledge of the way leading to the cessation of suffering—this is called right view.

"And what, friends, is right intention? Intention of renunciation, intention of non–ill will, and intention of non-cruelty—this is called right intention.

"And what, friends, is right speech? Abstaining from false speech, abstaining from malicious speech, abstaining from harsh speech, and abstaining from idle chatter—this is called right speech.

"And what, friends, is right action? Abstaining from killing living beings, abstaining from taking what is not given, and abstaining from misconduct in sensual pleasures—this is called right action.

"And what, friends, is right livelihood? Here a noble disciple, having abandoned wrong livelihood, earns his living by right livelihood—this is called right livelihood.

"And what, friends, is right effort? Here a *bhikkhu* awakens zeal for the nonarising of unarisen evil unskillful states, and he makes effort, arouses energy, exerts his mind, and strives. He awakens zeal for the abandoning of arisen evil unskillful states, and he makes effort, arouses energy, exerts his mind, and strives. He awakens zeal for the arising of unarisen skillful states, and he makes effort, arouses energy, exerts his mind, and strives. He awakens zeal for the continuance, nondisappearance, strengthening, increase, and fulfillment by development of arisen skillful states, and he makes effort, arouses energy, exerts his mind, and strives. This is called right effort.

"And what, friends, is right mindfulness? Here a *bhikkhu* abides contemplating the body as a body, ardent, fully aware, and mindful, having put away covetousness and grief for the world. He abides contemplating feelings as feelings, ardent, fully aware, and mindful, having put away covetousness and grief for the world. He abides contemplating mind as mind, ardent, fully aware, and mindful, having put away covetousness and grief for the world. He abides contemplating mind-objects as mind-objects, ardent, fully aware, and mindful, having put away covetousness and grief for the world. This is called right mindfulness.

"And what, friends, is right concentration? Here, quite secluded from sensual pleasures, secluded from unskillful states, a *bhikkhu* enters upon and abides in the first *jhana* [meditation], which is accompanied by applied and sustained thought, with rapture and pleasure born of seclusion. With the stilling of applied and sustained thought, he enters upon and abides in the second *jhana*, which has self-confidence and singleness of mind without applied and sustained thought, with rapture and pleasure born of concentration. With the fading away as well of rapture, he abides in equanimity, and mindful and fully aware, still feeling pleasure with the body, he enters upon and abides in the third *jhana*, on account of which noble ones announce: 'He has a pleasant abiding who has equanimity and is mindful.' With the abandoning of pleasure and pain, and with the previous disappearance of joy and grief, he enters upon and abides in the fourth *jhana*, which has neither-pain-nor-pleasure and purity of mindfulness due to equanimity. This is called right concentration.

"This is called the noble truth of the way leading to the cessation of suffering.

"At Benares, friends, in the Deer Park at Isipatana the Tathagata, accomplished and fully enlightened, set rolling the matchless Wheel of the Dhamma, which cannot be stopped by any recluse or brahmin or god or Mara or Brahma or anyone in the world—that is, the announcing, teaching, describing, establishing, revealing, expounding, and exhibiting of these Four Noble Truths."

Bhikkhu Nanamoli and Bhikkhu Bodhi, trans.

THE FOUNDATIONS OF MINDFULNESS (*SATIPATTHANA SUTTA*)

In The Foundations of Mindfulness, *the Buddha described in detail the methods of developing awareness that lead to liberation. This* sutta *is the basis from which Insight Meditation practice evolved. It is divided into four sections, one for each of the four foundations, indicated by subheads in capital letters, such as (*CONTEMPLATION OF THE BODY*), and subsections such as*

*(1. Mindfulness of Breathing) and (2. The Four Postures). Further,
within the four major sections there are brief presentations called
(INSIGHT), which summarize the key points in that section. The
structure and repetition of this format made the teachings, which
were transmitted orally, more accessible and easier to remember.*

1. THUS HAVE I HEARD. Once the Lord was staying among the
Kurus. There is a market-town of theirs called Kammasa-
dhamma. And there the Lord addressed the monks: "Monks!"
"Lord," they replied, and the Lord said:

"There is, monks, this one way to the purification of
beings, for the overcoming of sorrow and distress, for the disappearance of pain and sadness, for the gaining of the right
path, for the realisation of Nibbana:—that is to say the four
foundations of mindfulness.

"What are the four? Here, monks, a monk abides contemplating body as body, ardent, clearly aware and mindful, having
put aside hankering and fretting for the world; he abides contemplating feelings as feelings . . . ; he abides contemplating
mind as mind . . . ; he abides contemplating mind-objects as
mind-objects, ardent, clearly aware and mindful, having put
aside hankering and fretting for the world."

(CONTEMPLATION OF THE BODY)

(1. Mindfulness of Breathing)

2. "And how, monks, does a monk abide contemplating the
body as body? Here a monk, having gone into the forest, or to
the root of a tree, or to an empty place, sits down cross-legged,
holding his body erect, having established mindfulness before
him. Mindfully he breathes in, mindfully he breathes out.
Breathing in a long breath, he knows that he breathes in a long

breath, and breathing out a long breath, he knows that he breathes out a long breath. Breathing in a short breath, he knows that he breathes in a short breath, and breathing out a short breath, he knows that he breathes out a short breath. He trains himself, thinking: 'I will breathe in, conscious of the whole body.' He trains himself, thinking: 'I will breathe out, conscious of the whole body.' He trains himself, thinking: 'I will breathe in, calming the whole bodily process.' He trains himself, thinking: 'I will breathe out, calming the whole bodily process.' Just as a skilled turner, or his assistant, in making a long turn, knows that he is making a long turn, or in making a short turn, knows that he is making a short turn, so too a monk, in breathing in a long breath, knows that he breathes in a long breath . . . and so trains himself, thinking: 'I will breathe out, calming the whole bodily process.'"

(INSIGHT)
"He abides contemplating body as body internally, contemplating body as body externally, contemplating body as body both internally and externally. He abides contemplating arising phenomena in the body, he abides contemplating vanishing phenomena in the body, he abides contemplating both arising and vanishing phenomena in the body. Or else, mindfulness that 'there is body' is present to him just to the extent necessary for knowledge and awareness. And he abides independent, not clinging to anything in the world. And that, monks, is how a monk abides contemplating body as body."

(2. The Four Postures)

3. "Again, a monk, when walking, knows that he is walking, when standing, knows that he is standing, when sitting, knows that he is sitting, when lying down, knows that he is lying

down. In whatever way his body is disposed, he knows that that is how it is.

He abides contemplating body as body internally, externally, and both internally and externally. . . . And he abides independent, not clinging to anything in the world. And that, monks, is how a monk abides contemplating body as body."

(3. Clear Awareness)

4. "Again, a monk, when going forward or back, is clearly aware of what he is doing, in looking forward or back he is clearly aware of what he is doing, in bending and stretching he is clearly aware of what he is doing, in carrying his inner and outer robe and his bowl he is clearly aware of what he is doing, in eating, drinking, chewing and savouring he is clearly aware of what he is doing, in passing excrement or urine he is clearly aware of what he is doing, in walking, standing, sitting, falling asleep and waking up, in speaking or in staying silent, he is clearly aware of what he is doing.

"He abides contemplating body as body internally, externally, and both internally and externally . . . And he abides independent, not clinging to anything in the world. And that, monks, is how a monk abides contemplating body as body." . . .

(INSIGHT)

"He abides contemplating body as body internally, contemplating body as body externally, abides contemplating body as body both internally and externally. He abides contemplating arising phenomena in the body, contemplating vanishing phenomena in the body, he abides contemplating both arising and vanishing phenomena in the body. Or else, mindfulness that 'there is body' is present to him just to the extent necessary for knowledge and awareness. And he abides independent, not clinging to anything in the world. And that, monks, is how a monk abides contemplating body as body."

(CONTEMPLATION OF FEELINGS)
11. "And how, monks, does a monk abide contemplating feelings as feelings? Here, a monk feeling a pleasant feeling knows that he feels a pleasant feeling; feeling a painful feeling he knows that he feels a painful feeling; . . . feeling a feeling that is neither-painful-nor-pleasant he knows that he feels a feeling that is neither-painful-nor-pleasant; feeling a pleasant sensual feeling he knows that he feels a pleasant sensual feeling; feeling a pleasant non-sensual feeling he knows that he feels a pleasant non-sensual feeling; feeling a painful sensual feeling . . . ; feeling a painful non-sensual feeling . . . ; feeling a sensual feeling that is neither-painful-nor-pleasant . . . ; feeling a non-sensual feeling that is neither-painful-nor-pleasant, he knows that he feels a non-sensual feeling that is neither painful-nor-pleasant."

(INSIGHT)
"He abides contemplating feelings as feelings internally. He abides contemplating feelings as feelings externally. . . . He abides contemplating arising phenomena in the feelings, vanishing phenomena and both arising and vanishing phenomena in the feelings. Or else, mindfulness that 'there is feeling' is present to him just to the extent necessary for knowledge and awareness. And he abides independent, not clinging to anything in the world. And that, monks, is how a monk abides contemplating feelings as feelings."

(CONTEMPLATION OF MIND)
12. "And how, monks, does a monk abide contemplating mind as mind? Here, a monk knows a lustful mind as lustful, a mind free from lust as free from lust; a hating mind as hating, a mind

free from hate as free from hate; a deluded mind as deluded, an undeluded mind as undeluded; a contracted mind as contracted, a distracted mind as distracted; a developed mind as developed, an undeveloped mind as undeveloped; a surpassed mind as surpassed, an unsurpassed mind as unsurpassed; a concentrated mind as concentrated, an unconcentrated mind as unconcentrated; a liberated mind as liberated, an unliberated mind as unliberated."

(INSIGHT)
"He abides contemplating mind as mind internally. He abides contemplating mind as mind externally. . . . He abides contemplating arising phenomena in the mind. . . . Or else, mindfulness that 'there is mind' is present just to the extent necessary for knowledge and awareness. And he abides detached, not grasping at anything in the world. And that, monks, is how a monk abides contemplating mind as mind."

(CONTEMPLATION OF MIND-OBJECTS)
13. "And how, monks, does a monk abide contemplating mind-objects as mind-objects?"

(1. The Five Hindrances)

"Here, a monk abides contemplating mind-objects as mind-objects in respect of the five hindrances. How does he do so? Here, monks, if sensual desire is present in himself, a monk knows that it is present. If sensual desire is absent in himself, a monk knows that it is absent. And he knows how unarisen sensual desire comes to arise, and he knows how the abandonment of arisen sensual desire comes about, and he knows how the non-arising of the abandoned sensual desire in the future will come about.

"If ill-will is present in himself, a monk knows that it is

present. . . . And he knows how the non-arising of the abandoned ill-will in the future will come about.

"If sloth-and-torpor is present in himself, a monk knows that it is present. . . . And he knows how the non-arising of the abandoned sloth-and-torpor in the future will come about.

"If worry-and-flurry is present in himself, a monk knows that it is present. . . . And he knows how the non-arising of the abandoned worry-and-flurry in the future will come about.

"If doubt is present in himself, a monk knows that it is present. If doubt is absent in himself, he knows that it is absent. And he knows how unarisen doubt comes to arise, and he knows how the abandonment of arisen doubt comes about, and he knows how the non-arising of the abandoned doubt in the future will come about."

(INSIGHT)

"He abides contemplating mind-objects as mind-objects internally. . . . He abides contemplating arising phenomena in mind-objects. . . . Or else, mindfulness that 'there are mind-objects' is present just to the extent necessary for knowledge and awareness. And he abides detached, not grasping at anything in the world. And that, monks, is how a monk abides contemplating mind-objects as mind-objects in respect of the five hindrances." . . .

(2. The Five Aggregates)

14. "Again, monks, a monk abides contemplating mind-objects as mind-objects in respect of the five aggregates of grasping. How does he do so? Here, a monk thinks: 'Such is form, such the arising of form, such the disappearance of form; such is feeling, such the arising of feeling, such the disappearance of feeling; such is perception, such the arising of perception, such the disappearance of perception; such are the mental formations, such

the arising of the mental formations, such the disappearance of the mental formations; such is consciousness, such the arising of consciousness, such the disappearance of consciousness."

(INSIGHT)

"So he abides contemplating mind-objects as mind-objects internally. . . . And he abides detached, not grasping at anything in the world. And that, monks, is how a monk abides contemplating mind-objects as mind-objects in respect of the five aggregates of grasping."

(3. The Six Internal and External Sense-Bases)

15. "Again, monks, a monk abides contemplating mind-objects as mind-objects in respect of the six internal and external bases. How does he do so? Here a monk knows the eye, knows sight-objects, and he knows whatever fetter arises dependent on the two. And he knows how an unarisen fetter comes to arise, and he knows how the abandonment of an arisen fetter comes about, and he knows how the non-arising of the abandoned fetter in the future will come about. He knows the ear and he knows sounds. . . . He knows the nose and knows smells. . . . He knows the tongue and knows tastes. . . . He knows the body and knows tangibles. . . . He knows the mind and knows mind-objects, and he knows whatever fetter arises dependent on the two. And he knows how an unarisen fetter comes to arise, and he knows how the abandonment of an arisen fetter comes about, and he knows how the non-arising of the abandoned fetter in the future will come about.

(INSIGHT)

"So he abides contemplating mind-objects as mind-objects internally. . . . And he abides detached, not grasping at anything in the world. And that, monks, is how a monk abides contemplating mind-objects as mind-objects in respect of the six internal and external sense-bases."

(4. The Seven Factors of Enlightenment)

16. "Again, monks, a monk abides contemplating mind-objects as mind-objects in respect of the seven factors of enlightenment. How does he do so? Here, monks, if the enlightenment-factor of mindfulness is present in himself, a monk knows that it is present. If the enlightenment-factor of mindfulness is absent in himself, he knows that it is absent. And he knows how the unarisen enlightenment-factor of mindfulness comes to arise, and he knows how the complete development of the enlightenment-factor of mindfulness comes about. If the enlightenment-factor of investigation-of-states is present in himself. . . . If the enlightenment-factor of energy is present in himself. . . . If the enlightenment-factor of delight is present in himself. . . . If the enlightenment-factor of tranquillity is present in himself. . . . If the enlightenment-factor of concentration is present in himself. . . . If the enlightenment-factor of equanimity is present in himself, a monk knows that it is present. If the enlightenment-factor of equanimity is absent in himself, he knows that it is absent. And he knows how the unarisen enlightenment-factor of equanimity comes to arise, and he knows how the complete development of the enlightenment-factor of equanimity comes about."

(INSIGHT)

"He abides contemplating mind-objects as mind-objects internally. . . . And he abides detached, not grasping at anything in the world. And that, monks, is how a monk abides contemplating mind-objects as mind-objects in respect of the seven factors of enlightenment."

(5. The Four Noble Truths [see pages 191–196 for full text])

17. "Again, monks, a monk abides contemplating mind-objects as mind-objects in respect of the Four Noble Truths. How does he do so? Here, a monk knows as it really is: 'This is suffering'; he knows as it really is: 'This is the origin of suffering'; he knows as it really is: 'This is the cessation of suffering'; he knows as it really is: 'This is the way of practice leading to the cessation of suffering.'" . . .

21. "And what, monks, is the Noble Truth of the Way of Practice Leading to the Cessation of Suffering? It is just this Noble Eightfold Path, namely:—Right View, Right Thought; Right Speech, Right Action, Right Livelihood; Right Effort, Right Mindfulness, Right Concentration. . . ."

(INSIGHT)

"He abides contemplating mind-objects as mind-objects internally, contemplating mind-objects as mind-objects externally, contemplating mind-objects as mind-objects both internally and externally. He abides contemplating arising phenomena in mind-objects, he abides contemplating vanishing-phenomena in mind-objects, he abides contemplating both arising and vanishing phenomena in mind-objects. Or else, mindfulness that 'there are mind-objects' is present just to the extent necessary for knowledge and awareness. And he abides detached, not grasping at anything in the world. And that, monks, is how a monk abides contemplating mind-objects as mind-objects in respect of the Four Noble Truths."

(CONCLUSION)

22. "Whoever, monks, should practise these four foundations of mindfulness for just seven years may expect one of two results: either Arahantship in this life or, if there should be some sub-

strate left, the state of a Non-Returner. Let alone seven years—whoever should practise them for just six years . . . five years . . . , four years . . . , three years . . . , two years . . . , one year may expect one of two results . . . ; let alone one year—whoever should practise them for just seven months . . . , six months . . . , five months . . . , four months . . . , three months . . . , two months . . . , one month . . . , half a month may expect one of two results . . . ; let alone half a month—whoever should practise these four foundations of mindfulness for just one week may expect one of two results: either Arahantship in this life or, if there should be some substrate left, the state of a Non-Returner.

"It was said: 'There is, monks, this one way to the purification of beings, for the overcoming of sorrow and distress, for the disappearance of pain and sadness, for the gaining of the right path, for the realisation of Nibbana:—that is to say the four foundations of mindfulness,' and it is for this reason that it was said."

Thus the Lord spoke, and the monks rejoiced and were delighted at his words.

Maurice Walshe, trans.

THE HINDRANCES (*MAHA-ASSAPURA SUTTA*)

In this sutta, the Buddha described the five areas that most frequently cause us difficulties in our meditation—and life.

". . . Here, *bhikkhus*, a *bhikkhu* resorts to a secluded resting place: the forest, the root of a tree, a mountain, a ravine, a hillside cave, a charnel ground, a jungle thicket, an open space, a heap of straw.

"On returning from his almsround, after his meal he sits down, folding his legs crosswise, setting his body erect and establishing mindfulness before him. Abandoning covetousness for the world, he abides with a mind free from covetousness; he purifies his mind from covetousness. Abandoning ill will and hatred, he abides with a mind free from ill will, compassionate for the welfare of all living beings; he purifies his mind from ill will and hatred. Abandoning sloth and torpor, he abides free from sloth and torpor, percipient of light, mindful and fully aware; he purifies his mind from sloth and torpor. Abandoning restlessness and remorse, he abides unagitated with a mind inwardly peaceful; he purifies his mind from restlessness and remorse. Abandoning doubt, he abides having gone beyond doubt, unperplexed about skillful states; he purifies his mind from doubt.

"*Bhikkhus*, suppose a man were to take a loan and undertake business and his business were to succeed so that he could repay all the money of the old loan and there would remain enough extra to maintain a wife; then on considering this, he would be glad and full of joy. Or suppose a man were afflicted, suffering and gravely ill, and his food would not agree with him and his body had no strength, but later he would recover from the affliction and his food would agree with him and his body would regain strength; then on considering this, he would be glad and full of joy. Or suppose a man were imprisoned in a prisonhouse, but later he would be released from prison, safe and secure, with no loss to his property; then on considering this, he would be glad and full of joy. Or suppose a man were a slave, not self-dependent but dependent on others, unable to go where he wants, but later on he would be released from slavery, self-dependent, independent of others, a freed man able to go where he wants; then on considering this, he would be glad and full of joy. Or suppose a man with wealth and property were to enter a road across a desert, but later on he would cross over the desert, safe and secure, with no loss to his property; then on considering this, he would be glad and full of joy. So too, *bhikkhus,* when these five hindrances are unabandoned in himself, a *bhikkhu* sees them respectively as a debt, a disease, a prisonhouse, slavery, and a road across a desert. But when these five hindrances have been abandoned in himself, he sees that as freedom from debt, healthiness, release from prison, freedom from slavery, and a land of safety."

Bhikkhu Nanamoli and Bhikkhu Bodhi, trans.

LOVINGKINDNESS (*METTA SUTTA*)

One of the earliest concentration practices the Buddha taught was lovingkindness, which has proved to be an especially popular form of meditation among Insight Meditation students in the West.

This is what should be done
By those who are skilled in goodness,
And who know the path of peace:
Let them be able and upright,
Straightforward and gentle in speech.
Humble and not conceited,
Contented and easily satisfied.
Unburdened with duties and frugal in their ways.
Peaceful and calm, and wise and skillful,
Not proud and demanding in nature.
Let them not do the slightest thing
That the wise would later reprove.
Wishing: in gladness and in safety,
May all beings be at ease.
Whatever living beings there may be;
Whether they are weak or strong, omitting none,
The great or the mighty, medium, short or small,

The seen and the unseen,
Those living near and far away,
Those born and to-be-born—
May all beings be at ease!
Let none deceive another,
Or despise any being in any state.
Let none through anger or ill-will
Wish harm upon another.
Even as a mother protects with her life
Her child, her only child,
So with a boundless heart
Should one cherish all living beings;
Radiating kindness over the entire world:
Spreading upward to the skies,
And downward to the depths;
Outward and unbounded,
Freed from hatred and ill-will.
Whether standing or walking, seated or lying down,
Free from drowsiness,
One should sustain this recollection.
This is said to be the sublime abiding.
By not holding to fixed views,
The pure-hearted one, having clarity of vision,
Being freed from all sense desires,
Is not born again into this world.

Sharon Salzberg, trans.

....

From *The Dhammapada*

The Dhammapada *is a collection of sayings by the Buddha
that was transmitted orally until it was first recorded, in Pali,
in about the first century* B.C.E. *It remains especially popular*

among Theravada Buddhists in Asia and has gained in popularity in the West as a number of excellent translations have been published.

We are what we think.
All that we are arises with our thoughts.
With our thoughts we make the world.
Speak or act with an impure mind
And trouble will follow you
As the wheel follows the ox that draws the cart.

We are what we think.
All that we are arises with our thoughts.
With our thoughts we make the world.
Speak or act with a pure mind
And happiness will follow you
As your shadow, unshakable.

"Look how he abused me and beat me,
How he threw me down and robbed me."
Live with such thoughts and you live in hate.

"Look how he abused me and beat me,
How he threw me down and robbed me."
Abandon such thoughts, and live in love.

In this world
Hate never yet dispelled hate.
Only love dispels hate.
This is the law,
Ancient and inexhaustible.

You too shall pass away.
Knowing this, how can you quarrel?
How easily the wind overturns a frail tree.

Seek happiness in the senses,
Indulge in food and sleep,
And you too will be uprooted.

The wind cannot overturn a mountain.
Temptation cannot touch the man
Who is awake, strong and humble,
Who masters himself and minds the law.

. . .

An unreflecting mind is a poor roof.
Passion, like the rain, floods the house.
But if the roof is strong, there is shelter.

. . .

However many holy words you read,
However many you speak,
What good will they do you
If you do not act upon them?

. . .

Your worst enemy cannot harm you
As much as your own thoughts, unguarded.

But once mastered,
No one can help you as much,
Not even your father or your mother.

. . .

A Rendering by Thomas Byrom

14. Suggestions for Further Reading

Insight Meditation Practice and Teachings

Bodhi Bhikkhu. *The Noble Eightfold Path* (Kandy, Sri Lanka: Buddhist Publication Society, 1994). A wonderful and comprehensive description of the Eightfold Path.

Boorstein, Sylvia. *Don't Just Do Something, Sit There: A Mindfulness Retreat* (San Francisco: HarperSanFrancisco, 1996). The experience of meditation on a retreat, shared with practicality and down-to-earth humor.

———. *It's Easier Than You Think: The Buddhist Way to Happiness* (San Francisco: HarperSanFrancisco, 1995). A delightful presentation of major Buddhist teachings.

Boucher, Sandy. *Opening the Lotus: A Woman's Guide to Buddhism* (Boston: Beacon, 1997). An introduction to Insight Meditation with particular reference to the experiences and questions of women.

Goldstein, Joseph. *The Experience of Insight: A Simple and Direct Guide to Buddhist Meditation* (Boston: Shambhala, 1987). Unusually clear instructions on the practice of and hindrances to meditation by this master teacher and cofounder of the Insight Meditation Society in Barre, Massachusetts.

———. *Insight Meditation: The Practice of Freedom* (Boston: Shambhala, 1993). Succinct and clear essays on key aspects of Insight Meditation practice and how they can be integrated into daily life.

Goldstein, Joseph, and Jack Kornfield. *Seeking the Heart of Wisdom: The Path of Insight Meditation* (Boston: Shambhala, 1987). A rare blending of wisdom and practicality, presenting the keys to meditation and the practice of mindfulness, by two cofounders of the Insight Meditation Society in Barre, Massachusetts.

Gunaratana, Venerable Henepola. *Mindfulness in Plain English* (Boston: Wisdom Publications, 1991). A simple guide to Insight Meditation whose conversational style complements the depth of wisdom of Venerable Gunaratana's teachings.

Kornfield, Jack. *A Path with Heart: A Guide Through the Perils and Promises of Spiritual Life* (New York: Bantam Books, 1993). A practical and moving guide to living a spiritual life through the practices of Insight Meditation, by the founder of Spirit Rock Meditation Center in Woodacre, California, and cofounder of the Insight Meditation Society in Barre, Massachusetts.

Kornfield, Jack, and Paul Breiter, eds. *A Still Forest Pool: The Insight Meditation of Achaan Chah* (Wheaton, IL: Theosophical Publishing House, 1987). Wonderful stories and teachings that cut through delusions to the simplicity of truth.

Salzberg, Sharon. *Lovingkindness: The Revolutionary Art of Happiness* (Boston: Shambhala, 1995). This inspiring book by a cofounder of the Insight Meditation Society in Barre, Massachusetts, introduces the West to *metta*, or lovingkindness practice.

———. *A Heart as Wide as the World: Living with Mindfulness, Wisdom, and Compassion* (Boston: Shambhala, 1997). Stories, anecdotes, and brief teachings that show how to live this spiritual practice in the everyday world.

———, ed. *Voices of Insight* (Boston: Shambhala, 1999). A rich anthology of writings by teachers who lead retreats at the Insight Meditation Society.

U Pandita, Sayadaw. *In This Very Life: The Liberation Teachings of the Buddha* (Boston: Wisdom Publications, 1992). A traditional exposition of the Buddha's teachings that gives extensive details for practice.

....
Reference and Background

Kohn, Michel H., trans. *The Shambhala Dictionary of Buddhism and Zen* (Boston: Shambhala, 1991). Easily used alphabetical compilation of more than 1,500 terms and key historical figures in Buddhism.

Lorie, Peter, and Julie Foakes, compilers. *The Buddhist Directory* (Boston: Tuttle, 1997). A detailed listing of centers in North America and major centers in Europe.

Morreale, Don, ed. *The Complete Guide to Buddhist America* (Boston: Shambhala, 1998). Essays describing Buddhism and its major traditions in North America, as well as listings with descriptions of meditation centers.

Murcott, Susan. *The First Buddhist Women: Translations and Commentary on the Therigatha* (Berkeley, CA: Parallax Press, 1991). A fascinating compilation of the enlightenment verses of the earliest female disciples of the Buddha during his lifetime.

Nanamoli, Bhikkhu, and Bhikkhu Bodhi, trans. *The Middle Length Discourses of the Buddha* (Boston: Wisdom Publications, 1995). The authoritative translation of the 152 middle-length teachings, the *Majjhima Nikaya*.

Rahula, Walpola. *What the Buddha Taught* (New York: Grove Press, 1959). A classic presentation of the key concepts of Buddhism by a Buddhist monk and scholar.

Smith, Jean, ed. *Radiant Mind: Essential Buddhist Teachings and Texts* (New York: Riverhead, 1999). A compilation of key texts and commentaries selected for their accessibility to those new to Buddhism.

Snelling, John. *The Buddhist Handbook: A Complete Guide to Buddhist Schools, Teaching, Practice, and History* (Rochester, VT: Inner Traditions, 1991). Solid historical background as well as brief biographies of major teachers in the West.

Walshe, Maurice, trans. *Thus Have I Heard: The Long Discourses of the Buddha* (Boston: Wisdom Publications, 1987). The classic translation of the *Digha Nikaya*.

15. Insight Meditation Centers and Resources

Throughout the United States, the number of Buddhist centers for study and meditation has been growing rapidly. Those listed below exist at the time of this writing and are included to help you find an Insight Meditation center in your area; some are residential and some are not. Many of the centers have newsletters that can give you information about events sponsored by the center. Note, however, that temples that serve primarily the Thai community (identifiable as *wats*) and, in general, monasteries may have limited services available to the public or in English, so please check with these centers for their schedules. Buddhist magazines and the Internet also carry listings.

EASTERN UNITED STATES

Insight Meditation Society
1230 Pleasant Street
Barre, MA 01005
978-355-4378

Cambridge Insight Meditation
Center
331 Broadway
Cambridge, MA 02138
617-491-5070

Philadelphia Meditation Center
8 East Eagle Road
Havertown, PA 19083
610-853-8200
www.philadelphiameditation.org

Bhavana Society
Route 1, Box 218-3
High View, WV 26808
304-856-3241

Southern Dharma Retreat Center
1661 West Road
Hot Springs, NC 28743
828-622-7112
www.main.nc.us/SDRC

Bodhi Tree Dhamma Center
11355 Dauphin Avenue
Largo, FL 33778
727-392-7698

Dhamma Dena Meditation
Center
P.O. Box 76
Leeds, MA 01053
413-586-4915

New York Insight Meditation
Center
P.O. Box 1790, Murray Hill
Station
New York, NY 10156
917-441-0915
www.nyimc.org

Rhinebeck Insight Meditation
Group
141 Lamoree Road
Rhinebeck, NY 12572
914-876-7963

Forest Way Insight Meditation
Center
P.O. Box 491
Ruckersville, VA 22968
804-990-9300
www.forestway.org

Washington Buddhist Vihara
5017 16th Street N.W.
Washington, DC 20011
202-723-0773

Insight Meditation Community of
Washington
Washington, DC
301-562-7000

International Meditation Center
4920 Rose Drive
Westminster, MD 21158
410-346-7889

MIDWESTERN UNITED STATES

Dharma Center of Cincinnati
P.O. Box 23307
Cincinnati, OH 45223
513-281-6453

Mindfulness Meditation of
Columbus
P.O. Box 151534
Columbus, OH 43215
614-841-1908

Buddhadharma Meditation
Center
8910 Kingery Highway
Hinsdale, IL 60521
630-789-8866

The Grailville Sangha
932 O'Bannonville Road
Loveland, OH 45140
513-921-5377

American Buddhist Center
Unity Temple
707 West 47th Street
Kansas City, MO 64133
816-358-8353, ext. 143

Mid America Dharma
P.O. Box 414411
Kansas City, MO 64141
573-817-9942

Mindfulness Community of
Milwaukee
2126 East Locust Street
Milwaukee, WI 53211
414-962-8678

WESTERN UNITED STATES

Wat Dhamma Bhavana
738 West 72nd Avenue
Anchorage, AK 99518
907-344-9994

Mountain Stream Meditation
Center
P.O. Box 4362
Auburn, CA 95604
530-878-9485

Berkeley Thursday Night
Vipassana Group
Berkeley Buddhist Monastery
2304 McKinley
Berkeley, CA 94703
415-488-0164

Insight Meditation Community
The Yoga Workshop
2020 21st Street
Boulder, CO 80304

Insight Meditation Community
P.O. Box 5196
Bozeman, MT 59717
406-587-2755

Cloud Mountain Retreat Center
373 Agren Road
Castle Rock, WA 98611
888-465-9118
www.cloudmountain.org

Insight Meditation Dallas
P.O. Box 781632
Dallas, TX 75378
214-351-3789

The Lesbian Buddhist Sangha
4084 Lambert Road
El Sobrante, CA 94803
510-222-7787

Metta Meditation Center
401 South Fisher Street, #5
Glendale, CA 91205
818-543-0669

Vipassana Hawai'i
P.O. Box 240547
Honolulu, HI 96824
808-396-5888
www.vipassanahawaii.org

Hawai'i Insight Meditation Center
380 Portlock Road
Honolulu, HI 96825
808-395-5301
himc@vipassanahawaii.org

Dhamma Dena Desert Vipassana
Center
HC-1, Box 250
Joshua Tree, CA 92252
619-362-4815

Vipassana Metta Foundation
P.O. Box 1188
Kula-Maui, HI 96790
808-573-3450
www.maui.net/~metta

California Vipassana Center
P.O. Box 1167
North Fork, CA 93643
209-877-4386

Portland Vipassana Sangha
3434 S.W. Kelly
Portland, OR 97201
503-223-2214

Metta Foundation
310 N.W. Brynwood Lane
Portland, OR 97229
503-292-8550

Abhayagiri Buddhist Monastery
16201 Tomki Road
Redwood Valley, CA 95470
707-485-1630

San Diego Vipassana Meditation
    Society
1335 Santa Barbara Street
San Diego, CA 92107
619-225-0817

San Francisco Insight Meditation
    Group
1685 Union Street
San Francisco, CA 94123
415-979-4879

The Santa Fe Vipassana Sangha
96 Arroyo Hondo Road
Santa Fe, NM 87505
505-989-7610

Upaya
1404 Cerro Gordo Road
Santa Fe, NM 87501
505-986-8528
www.upaya.org

Seattle Insight Meditation
    Society
P.O. Box 95817
Seattle, WA 98145
206-336-2111
www.seattleinsight.com

Taos Mountain Sangha
    Meditation Center
P.O. Box 2854, Ranchos de Taos
Taos, NM 87557
505-737-2383

Tucson Community Meditation
    Center
2033 East Second Street
Tucson, AZ 85719
520-327-1695

Metta Forest Monastery
P.O. Box 1409
Valley Center, CA 92082
619-988-3474

Spirit Rock Meditation Center
P.O. Box 169, 5000 Sir Francis
    Drake Boulevard
Woodacre, CA 94973
415-488-0164
www.spiritrock.org

CANADA

Calgary Theravadin Meditation
    Society
3212 6th Street SW
Calgary, AB T2S 2M3
403-243-3433

Calgary Vipassana Meditation and
    Study Group
2017 42nd Avenue SW
Calgary, AB T2T 2M8
403-243-9697

Community of Mindful Living—
  Bow Valley Sangha
518 2nd Street
Canmore, AB T1W 2K5
403-678-2034

Eastern Canada Vipassana
  Foundation
C.P. 32083 Les Atriums
Montreal, QC H2L 4Y5
514-481-3504

Birken Forest Monastery
Box 992
Princeton, BC V0X 1W0
250-295-3263

Regina Insight Mediation
  Community
2275 Lorne Street #17
Regina, SK S4F 2M8
306-352-5691

Theravada Buddhist Community
136 Ellis Park Road
Toronto, ON M6S 2V5
416-462-4289

UNITED KINGDOM

Amaravati Buddhist Monastery
Great Gaddesden
Hemel Hempstead
Hertfordshire HP1 3BZ, England
44 (0)1442-842-455

Gaia House
West Ogwell, Newton Abbot
Devon TQ12 6EN, England
44 (0)1626-333-613
www.gn.apc.org/gaiahouse

OTHER RESOURCES

Study Centers

**Barre Center for Buddhist
  Studies**
149 Lockwood Road
Barre, MA 01005
978-355-2347
Academic courses of varying lengths

California Buddhist Vihara
American Buddhist Seminary
2717 Haste Street
Berkeley, CA 94704
510-845-4843
Degree programs for monastics

**California Institute of Integral
  Studies**
1453 Mission Street
San Francisco, CA 94103
415-575-6100
www.ciis.edu
Degree programs

Naropa University
2130 Arapahoe Avenue
Boulder, CO 80302
800-772-6951
www.naropa.edu
*Credit and noncredit programs;
  B.A., M.A., M.F.A., M.L.A.
  degrees*

Sharpham College
Ashprington
Totnes, Devon TQ9 7UT, England
44 (0)1803-732-521
www.sharpham-trust.org/
  sharpham
*Residential and residential one-term
  and one-year programs*

JOURNALS

Inquiring Mind
P.O. Box 9999
North Berkeley Station
CA 94709

Tricycle: The Buddhist Review
92 Vandam Street
New York, NY 10013
212-645-1143
www.tricycle.com

Turning Wheel
Buddhist Peace Fellowship
P.O. Box 4650T
Berkeley, CA 94704
510-525-8596
email: bpf@bpf.org
www.bpf.org

SELECTED WEB SITES

Dhamma Dena Meditation Center
www.dhammadena.org

Buddhist Peace Fellowship
email: bpf@bpf.org
www.bpf.org

Buddhist InfoWeb (DharmaNet)
www.dharmanet.org/infowebt.html

Buddhist Information Service of New York
www.infinite.org/bodhiline

Buddhist Studies WWW Virtual Library
www.ciolek.com/WWWVL-Buddhism.html
www.ciolek.com/WWWVL-Zen.html

AUDIO- AND VIDEOTAPES

Dharma Seed Tape Library
P.O. Box 66
Wendel Depot, MA 01380
1-800-969-SEED
www.dharmaseed.org

In Canada:
c/o Calgary Vipassana Meditation and Study Group
2017 42nd Avenue SW
Calgary, AB T2T 2M8
403-243-9697

Glossary of Selected Terms in Buddhism

aggregates (*skandhas* in Pali) the five components that constitute a human being: form (body); feeling (the quality of pleasantness, unpleasantness, or neither pleasantness nor unpleasantness); perception; mental formations (thoughts, emotions such as love and anger, and mindfulness); and consciousness (which arises when one of our senses makes contact with the world, so that there is visual, auditory, nasal, gustatory, tactile, or mind consciousness)

Ananda the Buddha's personal attendant, whose remarkable memory enabled him to recite all of the Buddha's discourses

anatta (Pali) selflessness or emptiness; absence of a permanent and unchanging self

Angulimara a vicious killer who wore a garland of his victims' fingers; he became a respected disciple of the Buddha after an encounter with him

anicca (Pali) impermanence

arahant ("worthy one," Pali; *arhat* in Sanskrit) a being who becomes free of all impurities of the heart and mind and attains Nirvana (*Nibbana*) at the end of this lifetime

Asoka the third-century B.C.E. Mauryan king of India who converted to Buddhism, changed India into a state based on the teachings of the Buddha, and convoked the Third Council

bare attention the kind of mindfulness that knows directly the essentials of an experience without interpretation, prejudice, or opinion

bhikku/bhikkhu ("monk" in Pali) the term for a monk in the Buddha's Sangha

Bodhgaya the town in northern India near which the Buddha became enlightened

bodhi tree a species of fig tree under which the Buddha meditated as he sought enlightenment

221

bodhisattva (Sanskrit) a being who seeks enlightenment in order to end the suffering and bring about the enlightenment of all other beings

Brahma-viharas. *See* **divine abodes**

Buddha ("Awakened One," Pali and Sanskrit) the historical figure probably born during the sixth century B.C.E. (563–483 B.C.E.?) into the Shakya clan, in what is now Nepal, and given the name Siddhartha Gautama (Sanskrit; Siddhatta Gotama, Pali); also known as the Shakyamuni Buddha ("the Buddha of the Shakya clan")

buddha ("awakened one," Pali and Sanskrit) a fully enlightened being

Buddha-nature, or **Buddha-mind** the fundamental nature and potential of human beings to become enlightened

Burmese posture the meditation posture with the heel of one foot near the pelvic area and the other leg folded in front of it, but not on top of it or crossing it

Ch'an the Chinese Buddhist sect believed founded in the sixth century, which became Zen Buddhism in Japan

compassion the "quivering of the heart" in response to pain and suffering

concentration the mind gathered and directed toward an object; one-pointedness of mind

dana ("gift," Pali) generosity; also refers to donations given to a teacher or given in support of the teachings

Deer Park the park in Benares (Sarnath, India) where the Buddha gave his first sermon, the Four Noble Truths

dependent origination the twelve links the Buddha used to describe the cycles of existence (*samsara*): ignorance, karmic formations (volitional actions, thoughts, and words), consciousness, mental and physical existence, the six sense organs, sense impressions, feeling (of pleasantness, unpleasantness, or neither pleasant nor unpleasant), craving, clinging, becoming, birth, death. The twelve links are not deterministic.

devas in Buddhist cosmology, celestial beings who live in heavenly realms but are subject to rebirth

Dhammapada an early collection of the Buddha's sayings in verse

Dharma (Sanskrit; *Dhamma* in Pali) Buddhist teachings; in the West, they are most often referred to by the Sanskrit term

Dharma talk a discourse exploring various aspects of Buddhist teachings and practice

divine abodes (*Brahma-viharas* in Pali and Sanskrit) absorptive meditation practice directed toward lovingkindness, compassion, sympathetic joy, and equanimity

dukkha (Pali) the quality of underlying stress, dissatisfaction, discomfort, and impatience that is part of everyday life and that can cause suffering when there is no wisdom; often translated as "suffering" or "dis-ease."

Eightfold Path the Fourth Noble Truth; the Buddha's teachings on how to end *dukkha* (suffering) through Right View, Right Intention, Right Speech, Right Action, Right Livelihood, Right Effort, Right Mindfulness, and Right Concentration

enlightenment a condition in which one sees into one's true nature and is free of all greed, hatred, and delusion; Nirvana

equanimity acceptance of how things are without grasping or aversion

factors of enlightenment the factors of mind that strengthen and come into balance as a condition for enlightenment: mindfulness, investigation, effort, rapture, tranquillity, concentration, and equanimity

First Council a gathering of five hundred elder disciples called by senior disciple Mahakashyapa approximately one month after the Buddha's death to affirm the Buddha's authentic teachings, which have come down as the Pali canon

First Noble Truth the teaching that *dukkha* (unsatisfactoriness) is the intrinsic nature of existence

Five Precepts Buddhist guidelines to live a life of nonharming: abstain from taking life, from taking what is not given, from false speech, from sexual misconduct, and from losing balance through taking intoxicants

Four Foundations of Mindfulness the Buddha's teaching on mindfulness of body, feeling (sensations of pleasantness and unpleasantness and neither pleasantness nor unpleasantness), mind factors (emotions), and mind objects (contents of thought; the core teachings of the Buddha), which lead to realizing Nirvana (*Nibbana*)

Four Noble Truths the heart of the Buddha's teaching—that *dukkha* is part of our lives; that it has a cause; that it can be ended; that the method for ending *dukkha* is the Eightfold Path

four qualities of the universe earth, air, fire, and water, which are experienced in the body as softness/pressure (earth), hot/cold (temperature), connectedness (water), and vibration (air)

Fourth Noble Truth the ending of *dukkha* is possible through the practice of the Eightfold Path

full lotus posture the cross-legged meditation posture in which each foot, sole upward, is placed on the thigh of the other leg

general comprehension the kind of mindfulness that knows in an inclusive way what we are doing and our purpose for doing it

half lotus posture the cross-legged meditation position in which one foot, sole up, is placed on the opposite thigh, and the other leg is folded in front of the body, with the foot tucked toward the pelvic area on the floor

Hinayana (Sanskrit) "Lesser Vehicle"; term applied to Theravada Buddhism by early Mahayana Buddhists

hindrances five qualities that challenge mindfulness and obscure our freedom: desire (clinging), ill will (aversion), sloth and torpor (drowsiness), restlessness (mental or physical), and doubt

insight the ability to see clearly things as they really are

Insight Meditation the name used in the West for Theravada Buddhism practice; also called Vipassana; the Buddha's practical teachings for awakening, which allow us to live without suffering

kalyanamitta (Pali) "spiritual friend," teacher

karma (Sanskrit; *kamma* in Pali) the relationship between cause and effect; the results of each of our conscious intentions through thoughts, words, and actions

koan a paradoxical phrase or story that transcends logic, most frequently used by teachers in the Rinzai Zen Buddhism tradition

Kusinara (Pali; Kushinagara in Sanskrit) the town in India where the Buddha is believed to have died, in 486 or 483 B.C.E., at the age of eighty, possibly of food poisoning

Mahakashyapa the senior monk at the time of the Buddha's death, who with five hundred *arahants* established an authoritative version of the Buddha's teachings

Mahayana the "Greater Vehicle" tradition, which encompasses both Zen and Tibetan Buddhism and stresses seeking enlightenment for all beings

Mara the embodiment of ignorance and its seductiveness; the personification of the hindrances

meditation cultivation of skillful qualities of mind, particularly mindfulness

metta (Pali) lovingkindness

Middle Way the balanced practice of mind and of body advocated by the Buddha; the path that avoids excessive sensual indulgence and excessive asceticism

mindfulness presence of mind or attentiveness to the present without "wobbling" or drifting away from experience

monk a renunciant who may live in a monastery; a *bhikkhu*

monkey mind the characteristic of the mind to jump from one thought to another to another

Nibbana. See **Nirvana**

Nirvana (Sanskrit; *Nibbana* in Pali) opening to the unconditioned or the highest peace with unshakable insight into the absence of "self," where there is no grasping, hatred, or delusion

Northern Transmission the initial spread of Buddhism to China, Korea, Vietnam, Japan, and Tibet

noting saying very softly in the mind words descriptive of what experience is arising, to support awareness during meditation

Pali an ancient language predating and similar to Sanskrit; the language in which the Buddha's teachings were first recorded

Pali canon the body of teachings of the Buddha affirmed immediately after his death, transmitted orally for several hundred years, then recorded in Pali; the central documents in *Theravada* Buddhism

perfections, or **ten perfections** (*paramitas* in Sanskrit) accumulated forces of purity within the mind: *dana*, or generosity; *sila*, or morality; renunciation; wisdom; energy; patience; truthfulness; resolution; *metta*, or lovingkindness; and equanimity. Siddhartha Gautama spent thousands of years, lifetime after lifetime, perfecting these qualities until he came to buddhahood.

Precepts. *See* **Five Precepts**

prostration a deep bow in which one begins standing, then kneels, bows and leans forward, extending the hands while simultaneously touching the forehead to the floor

Rahula the son of Siddhartha Gautama, who became the historical Buddha, and Yasodhara, his wife

Refuges. *See* **Three Refuges**

reincarnation the teaching in Theravada Buddhism that the positive and negative karma that we have created in our lives "jumps" when we have died into a new birth

retreat a temporary community where practice is supported by structured conditions such as silence; a retreat may last for a day or for many months

riding the horse the meditation position in which you place a cushion on edge between your legs and sit back on it

Right Action one link in the Eightfold Path; living according to the Five Precepts—refraining from taking life, from taking what is not given, from false speech, from sexual misconduct, and losing balance of mind from taking intoxicants

Right Concentration one link in the Eightfold Path; meditation; developing one-pointedness and skillful absorption for insight

Right Effort one link in the Eightfold Path; continually striving for mindfulness, especially in meditation; rousing will, making effort, exerting the mind, and striving, first, to prevent the arising and maintenance of unskillful states and, second, to awaken, enhance, and maintain skillful states "to the full perfection of development."

Right Intention (or **Right Thought**) one link in the Eightfold Path; renouncing ill will and cultivating *skillful* intentions; becoming aware of our thinking process; renouncing negative patterns of thought; and cultivating goodwill

Right Livelihood one link in the Eightfold Path; supporting ourselves through work that is legal and peaceful and entails no harm to others—specifically, work that does not involve trading in arms or lethal weapons, intoxicants or poisons, or killing animals

Right Mindfulness one link in the Eightfold Path; cultivating awareness of body, feelings, mind factors, and mind objects

Right Speech one link in the Eightfold Path; abstaining from false, malicious and harsh speech, and idle chatter; determining whether the time for speech is appropriate and whether it is both useful and truthful; speaking in a way that causes no harm

Right View (or Right Understanding) one link in the Eightfold Path; a thorough understanding of the Four Noble Truths, karma, and dependent origination

sadhu (Sanskrit) a wandering ascetic on a spiritual path

samadhi (Sanskrit) concentrated meditation practice; single-pointed focus bringing stability of mind

samsara ("cycles of existence," Sanskrit) journeying, day-to-day life in the cycle of ignorance and suffering

sangha (Sanskrit) spiritual community—originally a group of monks and nuns living under quite specific guidelines who are fully awakened, but now expanded to include novitiates, lay practitioners, and sometimes all who follow a Buddhist spiritual path

Second Council a gathering of senior monks, called about a hundred years after the Buddha's death, that reaffirmed the Buddha's teachings

Second Noble Truth the insight that the cause of *dukkha* (suffering) is grasping, greed, and the desire for things to be different from what they are

seiza **bench** a three-piece meditation bench with a slanted plank about eight inches wide and twelve inches long and two side planks about eight inches high

sense bases in Buddhism, eyes, ears, nose, tongue, body, and mind

Shakyamuni the "sage of the Shakya clan"; the historical Buddha

Siddhartha Gautama (Sanskrit; Siddhatta Gotama in Pali) the given name of the historical Buddha

sila (Pali; *shila* in Sanskrit) the term used primarily in Theravada Buddhism for "ethical action" or "morality," especially nonharming in speech, action, and livelihood

skandhas (Sanskrit) *See* **aggregates**

skillful leading to happiness, freedom, and awakening, without causing harm

Southern Transmission the initial spread of Buddhism to Southeast Asia

Suddhodana the ruler of the Sakya clan who was the father of the historical Buddha

sutra (Sanskrit; *sutta* in Pali) literally "thread"; a Buddhist discourse; in Theravada Buddhism, one of the Buddha's teachings collected in the Pali canon

sutta. *See* **sutra**

sympathetic joy taking delight in our own and others' successes

Tathagata (Pali, Sanskrit) the awakened one, the Buddha

Theravada ("Teaching of the Elders") the oldest Buddhist tradition, which exists in the West primarily as Insight Meditation or Vipassana; considered by some to be the most traditional stream of Buddhist teachings

Third Noble Truth the insight that there is an end to the cycle of dissatisfaction and suffering, and the possibility of enlightenment

Three Refuges taking refuge in the Buddha (or our potential to awaken); taking refuge in the Dharma (or the path that awakens); and taking refuge in the Sangha (or the community that practices this path); originally used as an expression of commitment to becoming a disciple of the Buddha

Tibetan Buddhism. *See* **Vajrayana**

unskillful causing harm and leading to suffering

Vajrayana (Sanskrit) the "Diamond Vehicle" school of northern Indian Buddhism, today found primarily in Tibet

Vipassana ("insight meditation," Pali) the stream in Theravada Buddhism also known in the West as Insight Meditation

vipassana ("insight meditation," Pali) meditation in which the nature of reality becomes clear

walking by counting a meditation practice in which you walk at a normal pace and count steps. When you take your first step, you count 1. On the next two steps, you say 1, 2. On the next three steps, you say 1, 2, 3. The next four steps are 1, 2, 3, 4, and so on all the way up to 10. When you reach 10, you say 10, then 10, 9 for the next two steps; then 10, 9, 8 for the next three steps, etc. Whenever you lose your concentration, you go back to 1.

walking meditation a formal meditation practice in which you walk back and forth between two points twenty to thirty feet apart. Usually you divide the walking meditation into three parts. During the first part, perhaps ten or fifteen minutes long, you walk a little more slowly than you would normally, focusing on stepping. During the second, also about ten or fifteen minutes long, you slow down even more, focusing on lifting and stepping. In the third, the remaining time you walk, you move quite slowly, focusing on lifting, stepping, and shifting the weight.

wheel of *samsara* mindless involvement in all the things that we do repeatedly without awareness

wisdom seeing what is skillful, appropriate, and timely; traditional Eightfold Path teachings of Right View, Right Understanding, and Right Intention

Yasodhara the wife of Siddhartha Gautama, who became the historical Buddha

zabuton a mat, about one and a half by three feet, used in meditation, often under a *zafu*

zafu a small, often round cushion used in meditation

zazen (literally, "seated mind") Zen Buddhist meditation

Zen (from the Sanskrit *dhyana* ["meditative absorption"], which was transliterated into *ch'an* in Chinese, then into *zenna*, or Zen, in Japanese) a major tradition within Mahayana Buddhism

....

Acknowledgments

Grateful acknowledgment is made for the use of the following:

ILLUSTRATIONS

Photographs on pages 178, 184: Abhayagiri Buddhist Monastery
Photographs on pages 19–21: Elizabeth Grace Burkhart
Photographs on pages 65, 177: Dhamma Dena Desert Vipassana Center
Photographs on pages 147, 180: Char Gentes
Photograph on page 17: Julia Moore
Photographs on page 238 (top): Frances K. Nkara
Photographs on pages 16, 27: Shelly Stevens
Photograph on page 169: Spirit Rock Archive
Photograph on page 179: Tim Wickens
Photograph on page 238 (bottom): Toni Dash
All other photographs by Jean Smith

TEXT

Excerpt on page 3 from *In the Words of Nelson Mandela*, reprinted by
    arrangement with Carol Publishing Group, Secaucus, NJ
Excerpt on pages 208–209 from *Lovingkindness: The Revolutionary Art of
    Happiness*, by Sharon Salzberg, © 1995. Reprinted by arrangement
    with Shambhala Publications, Boston
Excerpts on pages 196–205 © Maurice Walshe 1987, 1995. Reprinted
    from *Thus Have I Heard: The Long Discourses of the Buddha: A Transla-
    tion of the Digha Nikaya* with permission of Wisdom Publications, 199
    Elm St., Somerville MA 02144 U.S.A., www.wisdompubs.org
Excerpts on pages 191–196 and 206–208 © Bhikkhu Bodhi, 1995. Re-
    printed from *The Middle Length Discourses of the Buddha: A New Trans-
    lation of the Majjhima Nikaya* with permission of Wisdom Publications,
    199 Elm St., Somerville MA 02144 U.S.A., www.wisdompubs.org
Excerpt on page 47 reprinted by permission of Cynthia J. Embree-Lavoie
Excerpts on pages 209–211 from *The Dhammapada: The Sayings of the
    Buddha*, by Thomas Byrom, published by Alfred A. Knopf, 1976.

Index

Right Thought. *See* Right Intention

Right Understanding. *See* Right View

Right View, 81, 85–96

rites and rituals, attachment to, 76–77

Rose, Marcia, 180

Rosenberg, Larry, 179

Sakya clan, 52, 55

Salzberg, Sharon, 10, 64, 66, 138, 175, 208–209

samadhi. See concentration meditation

samsara, 13, 90

Sangha, 8, 9, 58–60, 166–168, 184, 189–190

Seattle Insight Meditation Society (Washington), 180

Second Council, 60, 182

Second Noble Truth, 72–78

Second Precept, 104–105

seiza bench. *See* bench

self-judgment, 110, 137, 153

sense bases, 203–203; sutta, 204

sensory pleasures, attachment to, 73–75

sensual desire. *See* desire

separation, 14, 55

seven factors of enlightenment, 117, 129, 130–132

sexual gratification, 109

sexual misconduct, 108–109

sickness. *See* illness

Siddhartha Gautama. *See* Buddha

Siddhatta Gotama. *See* Buddha

silence, 170

Silk Route, 63

sitting. *See* meditation

sitting in a chair posture, 21

skillful qualities, 11, 13, 33, 48, 56, 127

sleepiness. *See* drowsiness

sloth and torpor, 33, 42–43. *See also* drowsiness

Smith, Rodney, 180

Son (Korean Buddhism), 63

Southeast Asia, Buddhism in, 59, 61–62

Southern Transmission of Buddhism, 59, 61–62

Spirit Rock Meditation Center (California), 65, 166, 169, 178–179

Spirit Rock Teacher Collective, 179

Sri Lanka, Buddhism in, 62

story lines, personal, 41, 47, 90, 95, 115, 116, 126

Suddhodana, 52–53

suffering, 3, 4–5, 8, 11, 37, 57–58, 67–68, 83, 87, 115, 125, 147. *See also dukkha*

Sundari-Nanda, 124

suttas, selected, 191–209

Suzuki, D. T., 64

sympathetic joy, 148–151

Taoism, 63

Taos Mountain Sangha (New Mexico), 179–180

teachers, Buddhist, 8, 48, 71, 118, 162–166, 183, 187

Thailand, Buddhism in, 62

Theravada Buddhism, xi, 18, 25, 60–66, 156, 164, 182, 185, 186–187, 191. *See also* Insight Meditation

Thetgyi, Saya, 162

Tibetan Buddhism (Vajrayana), 60, 63, 164, 182, 183, 184

Thien (Vietnamese Buddhism), 63

Third Council, 61

A Note About the Authors

ARINNA WEISMAN is the lineage heir of Ruth Denison, one of the earliest women Vipassana teachers in the West. Arinna was a resident teacher at the Insight Meditation Society in Barre, Massachusetts, the first and largest Vipassana retreat center in the United States, and she has practiced for twenty years and taught for thirteen years throughout the United States and Europe. Born in South Africa, she leads retreats that focus on our capacity to transform ourselves through the practice of mindfulness and lovingkindness. She recently founded Dhamma Dena Meditation Center in Northampton, Massachusetts.

JEAN SMITH has more than thirty years' experience in publishing, most recently as a consultant, writer, and editor. For *Tricycle: The Buddhist Review,* she created a beginning Buddhist practice series—*Everyday Mind: 366 Reflections on the Buddhist Path* (1997); *Breath Sweeps Mind: A First Guide to Meditation Practice* (1998); and *Radiant Mind: Essential Buddhist Teachings and Texts* (1999). She has also published *365 Zen* (1999) and *The Beginner's Guide to Zen Buddhism* (2000). Jean lives with her companion *bodhisattva,* an Affenpinscher named Ani Metta, in a 120-year-old house in the Adirondack Mountains and also in Taos, New Mexico. She has been a Buddhist practitioner for many years and is a student of Arinna Weisman.

OTHER BELL TOWER BOOKS

....

Books that nourish the soul, illuminate the mind,
and speak directly to the heart

Rob Baker
PLANNING MEMORIAL CELEBRATIONS
....
A Sourcebook

A one-stop handbook for a situation more and more of us are
facing as we grow older. / 0-609-80404-9 • *Softcover*

Thomas Berry
THE GREAT WORK
....
Our Way into the Future

The grandfather of Deep Ecology teaches us how to move from
a human-centered view of the world to one focused on the
earth and all its inhabitants.

0-609-60525-9 • *Hardcover* / 0-609-80499-5 • *Softcover*

Cynthia Bourgeault
LOVE IS STRONGER THAN DEATH
....
The Mystical Union of Two Souls

Both the story of the incandescent love between two hermits
and a guidebook for those called to this path of soulwork.

0-609-60473-2 • *Hardcover*

Madeline Bruser
THE ART OF PRACTICING
....
Making Music from the Heart

A classic work on how to practice music that combines
meditative principles with information on body mechanics
and medicine. / 0-609-80177-5 • *Softcover*

Thomas Byrom
THE DHAMMAPADA: *The Sayings of the Buddha*

The first book in a series entitled "Sacred Teachings."

0-609-60888-6 • *Hardcover*

Marc David
NOURISHING WISDOM

A Mind/Body Approach to Nutrition and Well-Being

A book that advocates awareness in eating. / 0-517-88129-2 • *Softcover*

Joan Furman, M.S.N., R.N., and David McNabb
THE DYING TIME

Practical Wisdom for the Dying and Their Caregivers

A comprehensive guide, filled with physical, emotional, and spiritual advice. / 0-609-80003-5 • *Softcover*

Bernard Glassman
BEARING WITNESS

A Zen Master's Lessons in Making Peace

How Glassman started the Zen Peacemaker Order and what each of us can do to make peace in our hearts and in the world.

0-609-60061-3 • *Hardcover* / 0-609-80391-3 • *Softcover*

Bernard Glassman and Rick Fields
INSTRUCTIONS TO THE COOK

A Zen Master's Lessons in Living a Life that Matters

A distillation of Zen wisdom that can be used equally well as a manual on business or spiritual practice, cooking or life.

0-517-88829-7 • *Softcover*

Greg Johanson and Ron Kurtz
GRACE UNFOLDING

Psychotherapy in the Spirit of the Tao-te ching

The interaction of client and therapist illuminated through the gentle power and wisdom of Lao Tsu's ancient classic.

0-517-88130-6 • *Softcover*

Selected by Marcia and Jack Kelly
ONE HUNDRED GRACES: *Mealtime Blessings*

A collection of graces from many traditions, inscribed in calligraphy
reminiscent of the manuscripts of medieval Europe.

0-609-80093-0 • *Softcover*

Jack and Marcia Kelly
SANCTUARIES

*A Guide to Lodgings in Monasteries, Abbeys,
and Retreats of the United States*

For those in search of renewal and a little peace; described by the
New York Times as "the *Michelin Guide* of the retreat set."

0-517-88517-4 • *Softcover*

Stephen Levine
A YEAR TO LIVE

How to Live This Year As If It Were Your Last

Using the consciousness of our mortality to enter into a new and
vibrant relationship with life. / 0-609-80194-5 • *Softcover*

Helen M. Luke
OLD AGE

Journey into Simplicity

A classic text on how to age wisely by one of the great Jungian
analysts of our time. / 0-609-80590-8 • *Softcover*

SUCH STUFF AS DREAMS ARE MADE ON

The Autobiography and Journals of Helen M. Luke

A memoir, 140 pages culled from the 54 volumes of her journals, and
45 black-and-white photos—the summation of her life and work.

0-609-80589-4 • *Softcover*

Saki Santorelli
HEAL THY SELF

Lessons on Mindfulness in Medicine

An invitation to patients and health care professionals to bring
mindfulness into the crucible of the healing relationship.

0-609-60385-X • *Hardcover* / 0-609-80504-5 • *Softcover*

Jean Smith
THE BEGINNER'S GUIDE TO ZEN BUDDHISM

A comprehensive and easily accessible introduction that assumes no
prior knowledge of Zen Buddhism / 0-609-80466-9 • *Softcover*

James Thornton
A FIELD GUIDE TO THE SOUL

A Down-to-Earth Handbook of Spiritual Practice

In the tradition of *The Seat of the Soul, The Soul's Code,* and
Care of the Soul, a primer readers are calling "the Bible
for the new millennium."

0-609-60368-X • *Hardcover* / 0-609-80392-1 • *Softcover*

Michael Toms and Justine Willis Toms
TRUE WORK

Doing What You Love and Loving What You Do

Wisdom for the workplace from the husband-and-wife team of
NPR's weekly radio program New Dimensions.

0-609-80212-7 • *Softcover*

BUDDHA LAUGHING

A Tricycle *Book of Cartoons*

A marvelous opportunity for self-reflection for those who tend
to take themselves too seriously. / 0-609-80409-X • *Softcover*

Edited by Richard Whelan
SELF-RELIANCE

The Wisdom of Ralph Waldo Emerson
as Inspiration for Daily Living

A distillation of Emerson's spiritual writings
for contemporary readers. / 0-517-58512-X • *Softcover*